Imagination of the Heart

Imagination of the Heart

New Understandings in Preaching

Paul Scott Wilson

Abingdon Press • Nashville

IMAGINATION OF THE HEART
New Understandings in Preaching

This book is printed on acid-free paper.

Library of Congress Cataloging-in-Publication Data

WILSON, PAUL SCOTT, 1949-
  Imagination of the heart.
  Bibliography: p.
  1. Preaching. I. Title.
BV4211.2.W54 1988   251   88-14644

ISBN 0-687-18692-7 (pbk.: alk. paper)

MANUFACTURED BY THE PARTHENON PRESS AT
NASHVILLE, TENNESSEE, UNITED STATES OF AMERICA

To my teachers in preaching—

DAVID R. NEWMAN
CHARLES L. RICE
ANNA AND DONALD C. WILSON

ACKNOWLEDGMENTS

To my students, friends, and colleagues in various parish and college settings I am grateful for the many learnings I have received and which have contributed to this project. Particular thanks is due to those who worked through the manuscript in various stages: Phyllis D. Airhart, Glenn J. Ashford, Doris Jean Dyke, Bonnie Loewen, Frank Meadows, David R. Newman, Gerald T. Sheppard, Deanna L. Skeoch, Charles L. Rice, Thomas H. Troeger, Donald C. Wilson, and, somewhat later in the process, my editor at Abingdon, Rex D. Matthews. In addition to the value of their wisdom, their friendship and support have added pleasure to the task. Special thanks is also extended to members of the Monday "Lectionary Group"; to the congregation of First United Church, Port Credit, Ontario, who nurtured me as their pulpit supply minister during much of the writing of this book; to the Faculty of Religion at McGill University for the opportunity to test publicly some of my ideas; to the Academy of Homiletics whose members have regularly responded to and encouraged my writing; and to the Association of Theological Schools and the Board of Regents of Victoria University, University of Toronto, for grants to support a term's leave of absence.

CONTENTS

PREFACE

I n the northern conifer forests of the United States and Canada there are a variety of birds in the grouse family which seek winter shelter under the snow. Often when I have unknowingly walked too close to one's hiding place, I have been startled as it thundered up through the surface and past the tops of the trees. I have turned only to see a fine sunlit dusting of snow falling in its flight path. Sometimes imagination is startling and wonderful like that. I have been told, however, that many grouse die when freezing rain traps them under a thick crust. The imagination of many of us who preach may similarly be trapped. We need a way to set it free.

Homiletics is an exciting field which has developed rapidly in the last thirty years. It is now a discipline in its own right and enjoys widespread interdenominational sharing of resources and theory. One purpose of this book is to develop a method for biblical preaching that incorporates recent learnings from a variety of disciplines including homiletics. Another is to help preachers who share my own ongoing struggle to spread the wings of imagination when exploring the Bible.

This is written both for students in seminary and preachers serving churches. One of my courses in preaching is taught along the lines of this book and one week is devoted to the subject of each chapter here. Pastors in the field who want to use this book to renew their own preaching, or to learn how to preach in what may be a new style for them, may benefit from working on one chapter a week (or a month). Similarly, pastors wishing to teach laypeople how to preach might find helpful resources here. A subject index focusing on method is provided.

This book is intended to be ecumenical in scope. Since I teach in the largest federated theology school in North America my students are from many denominations, both Protestant and Roman Catholic. It is a time when we can benefit from conversations over denominational fences. I try to use the terms "sermon" and "homily" equally therefore, respecting that the former is Protestant and the latter is the preferred Roman Catholic term since Vatican II.

The approach presented here is new. Once the principles discussed in these pages are understood and learned, they can help reduce the time needed to prepare for preaching, improve the quality of the preaching, and can be easily adapted by those doing simpler forms of preaching, either for children or for daily services. I try to be comprehensive in the sense of giving detailed yet flexible guidelines for each stage of preparing a sermon or homily. Here is *a* method for preaching, not *the* method for preaching, for there can never be just one. The ones that most of us use are ultimately and wondrously quite personal, a combination of learnings from a variety of sources that we have found valuable. Fortunately, the value of any method for preaching is that is does not demand conformity but discloses opportunity.

At the same time the approach here is not simply a personal expression of how I approach preaching. It is based on principles I have found not only in Jesus' preaching but also in fine preaching (and books on preaching) throughout the ages. In homiletics the task of writing (or mentally preparing in a detailed way) for preaching has often been treated with ambivalence. More has been said around the task than about it. To help address this problem I offer the ideas presented here.

PAUL SCOTT WILSON
Emmanuel College
Toronto School of Theology

CHAPTER ONE

SUNDAY

Imagination's Poles

Whether from north or south, east, or west, most preachers have found themselves watching the church lot become empty after the service and asked themselves: "How can I talk about God's Word in ways more exciting for the people? How can I go on dealing with familiar texts week after week and remain excited myself?" When we ask these questions we are asking about many things: how to keep faith alive and vital; how to foster hope; how to keep our hearts open to our people; how to love them in a way that challenges and nurtures.

None of these is separate from the subject of what I will call imagination of the heart. It is one form of what we normally call simply imagination, but it is the form that is necessary for preaching. It is imagination illuminated by the Scriptures. It takes our experience of the world and shows us new possibilities. It opens mystery to us. It gives us the ability both to see this world as it is, with Christ in the midst of our brokenness, and to imagine a world different from our own, a world already transfigured by Christ's love, already penetrated by the new order. Imagination of the heart is always motivated by concerns of the heart, by God's love for the world, and by our desire to respond to that love.

Many people associate imagination with artists and think of it as a gift one either has or does not have. But much of what we consider as imagination or art is a skill. All musicians in the symphony are artists and have imagination. And all imagination involves mystery. But the best expression of imagination, the most powerful way of disclosing its mystery, comes from learning the techniques of the instruments. Musicians have studied theory. They have learned skills. They have practiced long hours; and when it comes time to play, no matter what the innate talent of the players, the wondrous sound that is produced in that moment of time is the product of years of accomplishment. They have learned their art.

Similarly, imagination of the heart uses skills that may be learned. Of course this imagination needed for preaching is rooted in faith. Though faith is a gift and cannot be learned, it is nonetheless intimately connected with imagination. Furthermore, the skills that imagination uses can be a means to deeper understanding of faith. Like the relationship between head and heart, imagination is inspired by faith and faith is strengthened by imagination.

Many preachers and would-be preachers have thought of imagination as some kind of mystical experience that is foreign and perhaps an experience to be avoided, hence they have not trained their imagination. Without this training, most preachers may be found in one of two camps. In the first camp belong those who assume they have imagination but have "no method for their madness"; they need procedural skills that will assist their own creativity for preaching.

In the second camp belong those who minimize their own imaginative abilities and concentrate instead on developing other skills, pastoral visitation or church administration perhaps; they need confidence to begin reaching out in new ways to the minds and hearts of their people. Common to all, however, is the fear of running dry, running out of ideas to preach.

When the words of the Bible come alive for today we see evidence of imagination of the heart. Even as a person may be faithful without a strong understanding of the faith, so too a preacher may have a strong understanding of the faith but may not have developed an imagination sufficiently to be able to stir the faith of others. We need training to be more creative. Someone with a well-trained imagination can be more effective than poetic genius who refuses training and constructive criticism. Moreover, as preachers, our primary instruments are our words and their delivery, and we want to use them well, as well as we can.

Training the imagination to create fresh ideas that intrigue only the mind is not enough. Highly abstract doctrinal reflection, of the sort that supports preaching in the form of systematic theology, requires imagination, as David Tracy makes abundantly clear in his *The Analogical Imagination* (Crossword, 1981). Preachers have an additional burden of using imagination to touch the heart and to stir the soul to action. To do this we need to become like Kierkegaard's subjective thinker: "While abstract thought seeks to understand the concrete abstractly, the subjective thinker has conversely to understand the abstract concretely . . . in terms of this particular human being."[1] Normally we do not associate our imagination with our heart. That is why it is helpful to use the phrase imagination of the heart in speaking about the imagination that reconciles heart and head, body and mind, in discerning God's purpose. In fact, it is precisely this formation of an interrelationship between two seemingly opposite concepts (like imagination and heart) that I will define as the action of imagination of the heart.

The phrase is, of course, biblical, although neither the phrase nor even the word *imagination* makes more than a cameo appearance in either Testament. It is the Noah story that speaks of the destruction of people who had evil in the "imagination of the thoughts of [the] heart." The blatant negative association need not prevent us from using it positively.[2] It is a sound hermeneutical principle to refuse to take biblical texts simply at face value and to turn them around to see what they say. If we do this, we find that the text also says that those who did not have evil in the imagination of their heart (Noah and his family) were saved.

The effect of imagination of the heart is neither peripheral nor ornamental. It touches the whole being. In Old Testament literature, the heart is understood as the seat of the emotions, the intellect, the will, and the spiritual life. "In fact, every survey of linguistic evidence has shown that there is hardly a spiritual process which could not be brought into some connection with the heart."[3] Knowledge in the Old Testament is never that of a disinterested viewer, the way in which our word *imagination* could imply some forms of intellectual detachment from the reality at hand. The heart is the place of personhood. When we use the phrase "imagination of the heart," we want it to retain something of the Hebrew sense of heart, therefore, of coming close to the ground of our being. It is an imagination that comes from the heart and goes to the heart.

Luther made a similar connection in linking the heart and the conscience. The conscience for him was the place in which God meets us. Imagination should be understood as a vehicle used by the Holy Spirit. In Greek understanding, the Holy Spirit always touches us to the core of our being.

As Gerhard Ebeling notes: "So the Holy Spirit, which is a new and renewing Spirit, creates a new heart, turns the 'heart of stone' into a 'heart of flesh.' That is, the Spirit awakes the heart and conscience . . . to real life from God and before God."[4] Our goal is to put our imagination at the total service of the Spirit.

This book is written to begin to meet the needs

of preachers and student preachers in both of the camps we named earlier: those who are creative without discipline and those who despair of ever being creative. It develops a detailed method that will help free the imagination in homiletical preparation. It is intended as a textbook for preaching. Using some of the approaches suggested here, preachers will find ways of tapping study and inner resources that will not run out, leaving them dry and barren. They will understand what it means when we say that a sermon or homily can begin to write itself. Imagination can become like the small supply of flour belonging to the widow with Elijah, flour that turned into a vast supply of bread (I Kings 17), or like the water at Cana turned into abundant fine wine (John 2).

The importance of imagination for good preaching has long been recognized. Henry Ward Beecher, who founded Yale's Lyman Beecher Lectures on Preaching in 1872, spoke of the imagination as "the most important of all the elements that go to make the preacher."[5] Ralph W. Sockman, giving the Beecher Lectures seventy years later, during World War II, was still calling on preachers to "sensitize" their "imaginations":

> When Sunday after Sunday a congregation prays to God . . . its imagination should be sharpened to see how life looks to the man in Ethiopia or along the Burma Road, in Berlin or in Coventry. That imagination which enables us to see what is justly due to another is pretty close to the quality of mercy.[6]

And George Buttrick is reported by one of his students to have said that, all other things being equal, "the better preacher will always be the one who has and uses the gift of imagination."[7]

Contemporary remarks about the importance of imagination for preaching indicate that its significance remains undiminished. The National Conference of Catholic Bishops (U.S.A.), reevaluating preaching for the post–Vatican II church, has said to Roman Catholic priests: "The more we can turn to the picture language of the poet and storyteller, the more we will be able to preach in a way that invites people to respond from the heart as well as from the mind."[8] The effect of this kind of picture language, says Fred B. Craddock, can be to give people an alternative way of life. Old life-denying images in the head may be replaced by life-affirming images in the heart: "This change takes time, because the longest trip a person takes is that from head to heart."[9] Charles Rice agrees, stressing that the burden to use imagination rests on preachers:

> Image evokes image, story calls forth story, life speaks to life. . . . But all of this depends upon the exegete/interpreter/preacher's capacity *to live in the symbol*, in this case in the very language and images of the text, to dwell in the house which the text provides. That capacity, an act of the imagination, is of the essence in forming sermons.[10]

There is wide and general concurrence on the importance of imagination for preaching. But there has been no such agreement as to how to prepare preachers to use this gift. Is imagination something we place over whatever style of preaching we have been following, in the manner we might overlay an additional transparency on

the overhead projector? Is imagination something intuitive that can only be learned with wide
reading and pastoral involvement, as Arndt
Halvorson and Edward Marquart suggest?[11] Is it
something one gains indirectly simply by telling
stories and listening to stories, as some popular
wisdom suggests? Or is it, as we will suggest here,
something that transforms our entire approach to
preaching and that needs to be cultivated one day
at a time, one step at a time, starting with the
significance of individual images and words and
moving up to what Ebeling called the completed
"word-event" *(wortgeschehen)*? The fact that
there has been no book devoted to how imagination works and how we might use that knowledge
to inform our preparation for preaching, even
though recently we have seen a sudden spurt in
the number of textbooks on preaching, suggests
the timeliness of the current task.

A number of recent developments suggest that
there is a shift taking place in biblical preaching
that amounts to a new emphasis on imagination
and a different understanding of it. One of these is
recent appreciation for the centrality of parable in
Jesus' teaching, as commented on for instance by
John D. Crossan, Sallie McFague, and Amos
Wilder. Another has to do with the emergence of
homiletics as an academic discipline in its own
right coupled with an apparent convergence of
thought in the work of some of the people who have
helped shape the new directions, people such as
Elizabeth Achtemeier, Charles Bartow, Frederick
Buechner, David Buttrick, Fred B. Craddock,
H. Grady Davis, Eugene L. Lowry, Morris J.
Niedenthal, Charles L. Rice, Edmund Steimle,

Thomas H. Troeger, Robert Waznak, and others.

A further development is the impact on preaching of literary criticism, hermeneutics and the phenomenology of language. Sermons and homilies may sometimes be described as having "a life of their own." They "grow," "move," and "flow," in a union of head and heart, intellect and emotion, logical appeal and evocative appeal. Form and content vary in accordance with the form and content of the biblical text. In short the sermon or homily is being upheld as a form of art dedicated to the opening up of God's living word for today. We could trace the seeds of this to William Wordsworth and Samuel Taylor Coleridge who helped revolutionize our approach to art. It was their idea that art has an organic unity—all the parts work together to form a unified total meaning. The poet should not start with a given structure or form like that of a sonnet and then add content as though the two are unrelated. Structure flows from content and content flows from structure: the two are inseparable.

David Buttrick argues moreover that preaching is a language of disclosure and that in preaching we are creating consciousness not simply exchanging information: "Thus preaching, as it forms faith consciousness, is a means of God's self-disclosure and saving grace *now*."[12] Current thought is also suggesting that the biblical sermon or homily not be structured primarily on the basis of logical argument and persuasion. Instead, it argues for plot or narrative direction, and, as in any good drama, character and emotion in addition to its rational appeal.

Because of this shift, many of the words we have

commonly used to talk about preaching no longer have exactly the same meaning for all preachers. For instance, to talk of building or constructing a sermon or homily may imply something quite different from shaping, molding, choreographing, or composing it. When we talk about structure now we no longer necessarily think primarily of points and sub-points, of outlines, of "introduction, body, and conclusion" or "openings, middles, and endings," and of thematic, doctrinal, or expository format. Or when we talk about story now we may no longer mean quite the same thing as illustration. These shifts in words are not casual or arbitrary. They indicate, like the tip of an iceberg that shows above the water, that something much larger exists at a deeper level.

Imagination has particular significance in all of this since the sermon or homily is being regarded as a form of art in itself. Not that it is ever merely art, or art for art's sake, or that the preacher's calling is to be highly inventive. The preacher's first and foremost task is simply to be a faithful witness to the scriptural word.

Rhetoric has always had close ties with homiletical theory. In the past the rhetorical emphasis has tended to be placed on the technical arts of delivery and style.[13] The preacher has been understood primarily as teacher or theological instructor, standing at the center of congregational life in the position of authority. Rhetorical methods have tended to be used to limit choices for the listener and to encourage responsible decision making. Imagination has been used to serve the purpose of the overall argument.

There currently is a movement in a different

direction, to enable and encourage participation
of the listeners. Within theology this is part of a
broader movement toward more contextual theology—theology rooted in the experience of
people in specific and varied cultural contexts.
Rhetorically, there may be more readiness to
understand what we do and what we effect when
we preach. There is also encouragement for the
preacher to resist the temptation to give answers,
to moralize or to lecture. And there is renewed
emphasis on sensitivity to language, on fresh
ideas in the biblical texts, and on careful
anticipation of the listener's thoughts and feelings. Here the preacher may stand "as one
without authority." Preaching may adopt the art
of Jesus' parables, inviting the hearers to participate, involving them in what is being proclaimed,
and looking for the completion of the preaching in
their own lives. What Sallie McFague says of the
parables may also be true of some sermons and
homilies: "They are not *primarily* concerned with
knowing but with doing."[14]

It is the additional purpose of this book,
therefore, to develop some guidelines for preaching that will assist those exploring current
homiletical developments. These guidelines pursue both preaching as it now is and as it might be
as it continues to develop. The methods for
assisting imagination given here never move far
from principles that Jesus understood and used in
his own preaching and that have been practiced,
although not named, by many biblical preachers
in ages past and present.

Nonetheless, guidelines for preaching should
always be understood as just that—guidelines,

not rules. They should be understood as supple, capable of being adopted, modified, and used in different ways. The Word of God and the way God speaks through our best and worst efforts can never be reduced to a discussion of our arts. The chief value of guidelines should be in providing suggestions that are important for what they provoke by way of response as much as for what they encourage through adherence.

At the same time, readers should not infer that the guidelines offered here are casual and arbitrary, as easily adopted as discarded. One problem with homiletical theory frequently in the past has been an absence of precise guidelines or, when there were guidelines, they had no theological rationale to support them. Ideas are sometimes adopted from communication theory or the latest trend in psychology without considering the implications for faith. The homiletical method here is rooted in theology and tries to define some principles that may be universal in homiletics.

General Theological Presuppositions

If we are correct in identifying a shift toward a more significant role for imagination in preaching, a shift fostered by new learnings about the parables, art, and the function of language, what does this say about our theology of preaching? For many people the connection of imagination with theology may seem unusual. It helps to remember that the preacher's imagination is leavened by both experience and the Scriptures. The preacher benefits from this union, and at the same time cannot do without it: preachers do not have the option of separating their imagination from the Bible. This dual regard for experience and scripture is what theology is, by definition. Thus while our overall task in this book is to present a method for preaching that can be followed by the parish pastor or the seminary student, it may also be understood more broadly as a method for doing theology. It is unfortunate that many of us have tended to think of the seminary alone, instead of the parish as well, as the primary place of doing theology in the church. Those who work faithfully at exegesis and at the relevance of biblical texts in the lives of people today, are theologians. Let me briefly list some additional theological presuppositions that inform this book.

1. *Preaching is God's Word, an offering of the incarnate Christ to the world.* In being God's Word, preaching, it is clear, is not the preacher's word, or the congregation's word, or the word of the world. The word of the world is so often a dead word which promises much yet leads to darkness. Because preaching is God's Word it is light. It is a living word. As Isaiah says, "The Word of God goes forth and it does not return empty or void." Walter Rauschenbusch, working with the poor in New York City, said that "God thinks in actions." God's Word is action. It is an event. It is the saving action of Christ through all the ages and through all time.

When we preach we participate in a unique way in God's salvation history. We break open the biblical text and allow God's Word to move out

into today's world with the same transforming
power and freshness as it held for the original
hearers. We preach as though someone's life
depended on it because someone's life does! As
Elizabeth Achtemeier has said more strongly,
"The eternal life or death of our people may
depend on their knowing what we mean."[15] The
words that we say are never identical to God's
Word nor can we ever be sure how the Holy Spirit
will use our words nor how they will be heard.

The objective truth of God's Word, Bonhoeffer
suggested in his lectures on preaching at Finken-
walde before Himmler closed the seminary, can
only be heard through the subjectivity of our
words.[16] We want, as much as is possible, to stand
out of the way of the biblical text, for our
authority for preaching comes from the Scriptures of the church. When we faithfully struggle
with the biblical text in study and prayer, when
we allow the Bible to interpret us as much as we
interpret the Bible, and when we faithfully
proclaim that Word we have experienced, God's
Word may be counted on to move through the
congregation and create that about which it
speaks.

2. *Preaching is a response to God's Word, an
offering of the preacher in service to God.* The
responsive nature of preaching can be understood
first in the restricted sense of preaching being a
specific command from Jesus: "Go into all the
world and preach the good news to all creation"
(Mark 16:15). "Response" also means that the
reason we preach is because God's Word in Christ
has encountered us and our lives have been
transformed by the Holy Spirit. Preaching is an

"awful" task, in the original sense of it being "full of awe." It is daunting to preach with the awareness that people listening to us are hearing God speak. No wonder students are often afraid of preaching. Woe to us if we ever lose that sense of awe.

Moses had perhaps the right attitude to preaching when he protested, "But who am I? . . . But who has sent me? . . . But they won't believe me. . . . But I'm not eloquent. . . . O my Lord, send I pray some other person." Who indeed are we that we might be worthy vessels for God's Word? We are not more righteous than the Pharisees or the Apostles and many of the fine preachers who have plotted the Christian route to our time, nor do we have to be.

Nonetheless we find ourselves called to preach. We do so not by any virtue of our own and not because we have a right. We offer ourselves to serve God in this particular manner because in our lives we have made choices that were inappropriate, we are sinners, *and* because we have experienced God's forgiveness and gift of salvation. By grace we have been deemed worthy in Christ. It is by the same gift of grace that we preach, allowing it to inform everything we say. And it is to that goal of proclaiming grace that we dedicate ourselves in studying preaching.

3. *Preaching is an offering of the people.* It is this in addition to being an offering of God and an offering of the preacher. As preachers, we do not stand against the people, untouched by their temptations or struggles. We stand *with* the people, as one of them, under the Word. The people are the church and they have set us apart for a particular kind of ministry, to bring their lives into focus before God. In this sense we could say that the "office" of preacher is part of their offering to God even as the entire worship service is their work of praise and thanksgiving, offered to God. We preach on their behalf. But their offering goes beyond this.

Protestants and Roman Catholics alike would agree with the Catholic *Decree of the Ministry and Life of Priests* in saying, "Preaching must not present God's Word in general and abstract fashion only, but it must apply the perennial truth of the gospel to the concrete circumstances of life." This application, however, might be understood in part the other way around. Our people's lives are as much an application of the gospel lived out in faith as they are the lives to which the gospel is applied. The preacher will gather up the events of the people as they have sought to live out their life's dedication to God, with all of the bumps and scratches, and will bring these lives forward before the Word. It will often be the particularity of their lives reflected in the preaching that enables individuals to rededicate their lives in the course of the worship service.

4. *Preaching takes place in the context of worship.* Something so obvious need scarcely be said, except that the implications are often overlooked. This means that the sermon or homily does not bear the entire weight of God's Word. God speaks through the prayers and hymns and all aspects of the service, but speaks in a particular and indispensable way in the opening up of the Scriptures for today and in the breaking of bread and the drinking of wine.

Similarly, neither sermon nor worship service as a whole stand on their own but stand in the context of the educational and healing ministries of the church. It is out of these that the worship arises, week by week, and it is to these that the worship returns. *No sermon or homily is over when it is delivered. It is completed in the life of the people throughout the week as they carry God's good news to the world.* Likewise no service is complete in itself. It flows from those services before it and into those that follow it as part of an unending celebration of the Christian year, year after year. Thus what is not said in the preaching may well be said in another way somewhere else in the service, and what is not said in one service as a whole perhaps may be trusted to another service. This may suggest the advisability of moving toward shorter sermons in some churches. The preaching is not able to make up for a weak educational program in the church. Preaching involves teaching but its primary purpose is not to teach but to invite people into faith.

5. *The responsibility for good preaching lies with both the people and the preacher.* Bonhoeffer spoke of the need for the congregation to listen with expectation, the expectation of encountering Christ. In other words, there is an appropriate attitude to bring to the hearing of preaching. This attitude will be enhanced if the preacher is a caring pastor, and if the congregation and preacher alike respect the time and study necessary for good preaching. Preparation time is to be honored as fully as we honor visiting the sick and shut-ins, or as fully as we honor preparing for the dinner guests, lest God's Word seem like reheated leftovers. In addition, preachers need and may want to encourage and honor feedback concerning the preaching. In this way preaching can become a genuine dialogue with the people, which anticipates their concerns and questions.[17] Adequate preparation time, combined with adequate steps of preparation, will help ensure that what Charles Bartow has called the "preaching moment" will never be a momentous task for the congregation to hear.[18]

How Imagination Works

To know how imagination works we need to know how language works, how words act together to produce meaning. I will be arguing here that imagination of the heart is not a mystical experience, although there is still mystery involved, but rather it is similar to other acts of meaning in the communication process. We may understand it as *the bringing together of two ideas that might not otherwise be connected and developing the creative energy they generate.* Normally, however, we may not think of imagination as having anything to do with language. We may think of it as the ability to picture something and may connect it more with vision than with words. This needs to change. Imagination may at times be a kind of wordless mystery that will involve pictures or other forms of mental sensory images. And pictorial imagery may at times enable us to find words, as Ignatian meditation exercises suggest. But in general we may understand that imagination is released by an ability to use polarities in language to create fresh ideas. Many of these ideas will present pictures to the mind, but imagination that finds expression through words is essentially a function of language. Without language we are unable to express thought. It is through the windows of language that we view reality, that we interpret actions, that we understand our emotions and our faith. The subject is a difficult one, however, and it may be useful, before going into some of the scholarship in the area, for us to resort to pictures to show how imagination functions.

There are two ways in which it might be helpful for us to picture how imagination works. One way is to consider a close personal relationship like a marriage. In a marriage that works well, both people are confident in their own individual identities. If one person becomes lost in the identity of the other, much of the spark of the relationship may be gone. But if the partners, while being committed to each other, support individual growth and identity, the spark will be maintained. What we have here are three identities: the two individual identities and the third identity that is the relationship itself. It is characterized by the way the couple behaves as a couple. If this relationship is strong, we might say that there is a spark between them. Imagination in language is like this kind of vital relationship, except that in language it is two ideas brought together, each with its own identity, to create a third new identity by their union.

From my senior physics class in high school comes a second way of picturing how imagination works. The teacher had brought out an old generator. Taken from an old farmhouse telephone, it was the kind that had to be cranked by hand. Both the negative and positive poles of the generator had a wire attached. A student kept cranking while the teacher brought the ends of the two wires closer and closer together. When the ends were six inches apart, a spark jumped through the air with a snap. When the ends were four inches apart there was a crackling sound and a waving but constant spark between the two ends. When the wires were touching there was no visible spark although the current was flowing.

Imagination in language is like this spark between the poles of the generator. The spark of imagination happens when two ideas that seem to have no apparent connection (standing "poles apart," we might say) are brought together. Two conditions are necessary for imagination: (1) some connection between the ideas must be possible and (2) the ideas chosen must not be almost identical, for then they would function like the touching wires that had no visible spark. Most acts of communication happen with the wires touching and the current of meaning flowing directly from one idea to another with little or no spark visible.

Part of my own excitement about these ideas is the support they receive from a variety of disciplines. For instance, Samuel Taylor Coleridge, the poet who built his entire philosophy around imagination in his *Biographia Literaria* (1817), called imagination the "reconciliation of opposites." Many of his critics thought he meant literal reconciliation of logical opposites, each of which was in effect neutralized or negated. Rather he meant a bringing together of separate identities to produce a new meaning.[19] Whenever there was imagination or creativity present, he argued, it was because two "opposites" had been "reconciled," like two powerful horses straining against each other in harness, yet each pulling to a common purpose. While "reconciliation of opposites" was Coleridge's phrase, it may be helpful for us also to speak of juxtaposition of opposites or tension between opposites to remind us how imagination works.

A wide variety of interpretations have been given to imagination from Aristotle onward. These interpretations are complex and vary from considering imagination as one of the human faculties (along with, for instance, understanding and reason) to an ability to see in pictures. For us, however, it is the work that some individuals have devoted to how meaning is produced in language that is most relevant to the central point here—that imagination in general and meaning in particular are the result of poles in language interacting.

Many people have argued that meaning in language is the result of mediation between opposites. For instance it was Hegel's notion that "determination is negation," implying that we can only define what something is by showing what it is not: what it means becomes clear in relationship to something else, or in other words, in the interaction between the two. C. S. Pierce, a philosopher whose theories of communication are now at the forefront of language research, has suggested that in any language system, meaning is produced by a threefold process almost identical to Coleridge's discussion of imagination. This process involves: (1) immediacy, or what we have been calling identity, (2) opposition, and (3) mediation.[20]

Walter Ong, Max Black, Paul Ricoeur, Sallie McFague, and many others have argued that metaphor is an act of meaning similar in structure to other acts of "meaning."[21] Roman Jakobson, in a classic study on children, was able to establish that we learn the meaning of language only by thinking in terms of opposites like "bad" and "good" (what he called "binary opposites").[22] Levi-Strauss' study of myths led him to conclude that no matter how varied the characters of cultures of different myths, their meanings were determined by basic oppositions such as sun/moon, day/night, mother/daughter, man/woman, brother/stepbrother, that control the structure of myths.[23] Terry Eagleton puts the matter succinctly: "Binary oppositions are devices to think with, ways of classifying and organizing reality, and this, rather than the recounting of any particular tale, is their point."[24] And A. J. Greimas and numerous others have modified further the fundamental principle of the fields of semiotics and structuralism: that all meaning is relational.[25]

All these writers are saying what we as Christians have known for a long time in terms of personal relationships, that fulfillment and meaning in life cannot exist in isolation from others. The meaning of individual life, like the meaning of language, is relational and found in the context of relationships.

Imagination similarly is the product of two ideas or "opposites" in relationship. The case that is being made here is that imagination operates in language, not just in pictures outside of language. Metaphor is language that exercises imagination. Imagination is not something magical or mysterious and unknown, even though its effect may seem both magical and mysterious. We have to know this if we are ever going to trust our creative abilities. As long as we cast an air of total mystique around imagination, we will assign it to the unknowable and thus also to the unachievable.

Using Imagination with Individual Words

Let us begin to pursue how we as preachers may use imagination. Our starting point is with individual words. What do the above theories of meaning and imagination imply for individual words?

There is a way in which we may understand that most of the words in any language are the result of mediation between two separate "identities." We need not argue this in detail here: this has already been established in the discipline known as semiotics. Nor is it our purpose to do more than point out that even when words are formed of sound and concept, we have "opposites" interacting.

Let us assume that we do not yet have language and that a sound like "rrawk" is connected with the object we call "rock." We have a *sound* or what Paul Ricoeur calls an "acoustic image" of "rrawk"; this is the first identity. We connect the sound with the *concept* of "the hard object"; this is the second identity and stands in tension or opposition with the first. In connecting or juxtaposing the two we form the repeatable linguistic *sign* of "rock," which we are able to transfer to other similar "hard objects"; this is the third identity that may be said to mediate between the first two.[26]

What particular *sign* we settle on to communicate an idea is of course generally arbitrary; there is no inherent reason for a rock to be called a "rock," a sink a "sink," or a cat a "cat." If this were not arbitrary, surely a cat would be called a "meow" and a car would be called a "varoom," as children sometimes say. What matters is that in a particular culture we agree on the chosen sign. There is a sense then, in which most of our words are the result of mediation between opposites. Said another way, most words have a metaphoric or tensive quality to them.

From a more practical point of view for preaching, mediation between opposites is readily apparent if we look at another level of words. Many of our words actually contain two ideas within them. The word "weary," for instance, originally meant "to walk over wet ground." The meaning of the word was produced by the mediation between "to walk" and "wet ground," even though we think of it now as one idea meaning "tired."

Similarly the root of "to learn" combines "to follow" and "a track"; "lunacy" combines "insanity" and "phase of the moon"; the root of "transgression" combines "to cross" and "a line"; "communion" combines "to share" and "in common"; "companion" combines "to share" and "bread"; and "ecclesia" combines "to call" and "assemble." The list could go on indefinitely, and, with a little exploring in a good dictionary, we could each supply the original sources for some of our words.

The point here is that we have lost sight of the original act of mediation performed in many of our words. We simply connect the words with the one thing we think they mean: thus transgression means sin, and communion means sacrament. In the process other meanings tend to be lost. This process is natural and important because it streamlines the language and enables us to communicate a great deal of information quickly. But as in our picture of the telephone generator with the wires touching, the electric current may still be flowing but there is no spark to be seen. There is meaning without imagination.

To use imagination with language of this sort, *often what we need to do is to rediscover the original poles, to put the "opposites" back into some words*, to take our people to the sources of particular words in our preaching in exciting ways. Each of us can probably recall a time when the discovery of the root meaning of a particular word caught the imagination and opened up a new range of thoughts and feelings. By recovering the origins of some words we have one small way of using imagination for more powerful preaching.

Perhaps even more important for imagination than this, however, is the understanding that language lives and language dies. The reason it is more important we will see in a moment. Whenever words lose some of their spark for us they have died a little. We experience this kind of death in language when a favorite tune on the radio becomes a matter of indifference; or when in worship the same phrase used week after week without variation ceases to have meaning for us; or when an idea that was fresh and alive for us at a conference becomes dry and shriveled when left forgotten in a drawer for months.

The decay of meaning in language is predictable. This can lead, as noted already, to streamlining language and to effective communication. On the other hand it can eventually lead to dropping entire words from our vocabulary. Anthropologists working with the Inuit people in the North American Arctic have actually used this predictable process of decay in language to help them date the origin of some of the isolated communities; assuming that these communities have a common origin, they suggest that every one hundred years they lose half of the words they have in common as new words are invented to replace the old. In 1986 some Canadian Inuit were brought together for the first time with some Russian Inuit, and it was discovered that they still had some words in common. Readers who know basic physics may find it helpful to think of the decay of meaning in language as being similar to the decay of radioactive isotopes according to their particular half-lives.

The decay of language is important for preachers to understand, particularly those who are learning to use the imagination. Quite simply, many of the words we commonly use to talk about the faith have lost their spark. Repeated use of them without exposing them to imagination will have no more positive effect on the congregation than will raising the voice in giving directions to someone who does not speak our language. As Edward F. Marquart has identified the problem:

> Most of the laity do not have "gut associations" with such words as salvation, redemption, incar-

nation, gospel, and theology of the cross. Ninety-
eight percent of our laity don't use these words in
their everyday lives. This becomes a problem for
many of us clergy because we all have our
favorite words. . . . [Someone] said to Reuel
Howe, "If I used that much jargon with my
customers, I would lose them."[27]

Too many of our big theological words seem to
our people like a lost herd of cattle out on the back
forty. The solution is not just to cut back on the
use of these words: jargon is still jargon used once
or one hundred times. Nor is the solution to
eliminate them entirely from our preaching. *The
words of the Christian faith are gifts to us. They are
treasures of which we are the stewards: We cannot
let them die for they can be the route to true life.* The
solution then must lie in another direction.

The solution has to do with language renewal.
Just as words can decay and die, so too can they be
renewed and have fresh life. The words of our
faith are precious, yet they sometimes litter the
floor like unthreshed husks of wheat. Some people
would tread on them underfoot. For them the
words are dead; they may have heard the words
but they never received them as life. When these
same words are gathered up with care and
thrown into the air, the Holy Spirit has a chance
to blow through them, to winnow them, to sift out
the good news anew. They are renewed when they
are seen or heard as though for the first time,
when they have life again, when people want to
use them because they have again become
important for them.

Language renewal is not the task of a few. It is
the task of everyone in the church, but it is the

particular task of preachers. Said quite starkly, *language renewal is faith renewal.* Faith can be renewed by actions, but faith seeks understanding, and understanding comes from words and ideas.

Perhaps it would be better for some people in our society to have never heard about the Christian faith than to have the distorted understanding of it that they have. For them in particular, and for many of our church regulars as well, new ways to understand old words are essential. Because we love the words of our faith, and because we love to use them well and hear them well used, we take care of them. We want to polish them in all of their natural beauty like restored wood, so that others may run their fingers along the contours and know God's truth.

How does imagination give back to us with freshness some of our words that are worn out and coming apart at the seams? As noted, retracing the origin of many of our words and recreating opposition is one route. Another is to reach outside of the word itself to create a new opposition or juxtaposition. Let us say that we are wanting to use the word "salvation" in a new way. For imagination we need to have what Coleridge called the reconciliation of opposites. We need two poles and we already have one in the word "salvation." Like the wires of the generator, the "opposites" cannot be so far apart that no connection is possible and yet cannot be so close together that they are touching. "Salvation" can have no legitimate connection, for instance, with "bomb." There is a false connection, of course, of the sort we find in so many of the false salvation promises of our culture such as in the lotteries and the life-style beer advertisements. But since no relationship of truth can be established with "bomb," there can be no spark of imagination of the heart. The wires are held too far apart. Imagination of the heart is scripturally based and the spark must have biblical warrant.

Or again, there can be no spark if the ideas are so similar that the wires are touching: the words "salvation" and "redemption" are so similar as to be almost identical. The preacher who talks about salvation as redemption will catch a lot of the congregation snoozing. But if the preacher tries substituting another word to juxtapose with salvation, a spark with biblical warrant may be found. Salvation can imply a positive experience. There are many positive experiences that might be effective, but one obvious one for Christians might be eating a meal. Bring that experience alongside the word "salvation" and there will be a spark that opens fresh and yet familiar biblical horizons for faith: "salvation is eating a meal." A congregation would be interested to hear the preacher develop this idea.

Of course this is only one instance of imagination or reconciliation of opposites. We could create many more with a word like "salvation." Simply try substituting any number of other positive experiences in place of eating a meal. But since salvation is inseparable from the cross, we might want alternately to try some other fresh juxtapositions that we could develop in our preaching, such words as "cross," "electric chair," "humiliation," or "vulnerability." Obviously in developing some of these for preaching we would need to be careful not to justify the suffering and oppression God opposes so clearly in the Scriptures. Moreover, we need not use every one. But as Arthur Koestler noted over and over again in his *Act of Creation*,[28] the imaginative breakthroughs of creative people have occurred because of their ability to go beyond the usual frameworks of their disciplines and to associate ideas in unusual ways.

It takes no genius to play with free association. For us it can be an act of freedom. Part of the process can be a creative mulling, even without words, using music or art to awaken non-discursive realities, before we move to words. But when we move to words, do not dismiss apparently inappropriate juxtapositions before mulling them over in your mind. *Too often we cut off our considerable creative talents because we jump in too quickly to try to evaluate theological truth. As Jesus said in one of the parables, let the seeds grow and then do the weeding.* Ask yourself, "Is there a way this might be true?"

To be creative we need to be willing to live long enough with the tension between ideas to be able to explore freely. Even though not every juxtaposition will be appropriate, there will be a few we could develop and elaborate in preaching. We simply keep free-associating and substituting until something is alive for us.

It was Paul Ricoeur who said of metaphor that it both "is" and "is not." And clearly when we are creating the juxtaposition of opposites in this way we are creating metaphors. In trusting our imagination and that of our hearers, we need not pay undue attention to the "is not"—the way in which for instance salvation is not like eating a meal. The "is not" frequently is what we bring to a juxtaposition of opposites because our literal way of thinking tends immediately to say, "It cannot be. It is not. The two are not identical." Instead we trust that the context of our remarks in the preaching, or our own brief words of elaboration, will sufficiently develop the *is* for the congregation to say its own yes and no.

Creating opposites, either from within the origin of individual words or by bringing one word or idea alongside another, is to begin to see the power of imagination. As preachers we must start with individual words; later on we will be discussing how individual words can function as one-word stories. Once we see how juxtaposition is done, we can see how others have created in exciting ways. For example, when Frederick Buechner said that it was harder for a rich person to enter the Realm of God than for a Mercedes to go through a revolving door,[29] he probably used this process of free-associating and substitution of individual words. As a substitute for "camel" he settled on "Mercedes" (what do rich people ride in today?) and as a substitute for "eye of a needle" he settled on "revolving door" (which a car would have difficulty going through). The reconciliation of these two ideas of "Mercedes" and "revolving door" is an example of imagination.

Imagination creates new windows in language for us, opens up new possibilities of faith for us, gives us new eyes with which to view the world, and gives us new words with which to proclaim the glory of Christ. Is this not also the task of preaching in the life of the church? Preaching renews the language of the faith, even as it preserves and perpetuates it.

The instances we have been looking at in relation to individual words are the most basic level of imagination for preaching. There are, of course, many other levels beyond individual words on which it is necessary to use imagination if our preaching is to be powerful. We will be turning to these in a moment.

I have been saying that imagination exists because of the juxtaposition of opposites. If our preaching is to demonstrate imagination our approach must be to build in certain polarities or opposites. What are these polarities for preaching? What juxtapositions will ensure that scriptural truth will be given first priority in our preaching? There are many paired opposites that we could focus on to assist imagination in preaching. Here we will concentrate on four of the most basic which have universal implications for preaching. They help identify what biblical preaching needs to contain and they cover much of the preaching waterfront: (1) the biblical text and our situation, (2) law and gospel (or judgment and grace), (3) story and doctrine, and (4) pastor and prophet.[30]

Another way of thinking about these polarities is to understand that each is concentrating on different levels of the preaching text: under "biblical text and our situation" we will juxtapose groups of words—a way of allowing the biblical text to shape our written sermon or homily; under "law and gospel" we will juxtapose key theological ideas for preaching—a way to determine the central idea of the sermon or homily and give direction to the preaching; with "story and doctrine" we will juxtapose the two ancient forms or ways of theological expression—a way of addressing all our people; and with "pastor and prophet" we will juxtapose the two missions of preaching.

Yet another way of understanding these polarities is to recognize that each tries to address or solve a specific and chronic problem in preaching today: the problem of making preaching both biblical and relevant, the problem of preaching that offers little good news, the problem of ensuring that our preaching is accessible to the entire congregation, and the problem of dealing with tough issues in preaching. This book is written so that each chapter builds on what went before, but preachers seeking help with a specific problem may simply turn to the relevant chapter.

In each of the chapters, the basic dynamic will be the same. Juxtapose two identities in order to create a spark that will be rooted in scripture. It is natural when learning a new way of doing something to want to ask, "What will this look like in the final product?" Particularly in the early stages this can interfere with the learning process. If we tend to each level, one at a time, and concentrate on learning a little at a time, we will find that the process of using imagination is attainable for every preacher, including ourselves.

Our task now is to show how imagination may be released. In the chapters ahead we will look at each of the levels in turn, assigning one day or group of days to each level, starting at the beginning of the preacher's week and progressing through to Sunday. The intent here is to provide one way of incorporating the necessary elements for imaginative preaching. What is written about here has to happen, but it may happen no doubt in many other ways. Similarly, the intent is that preachers will feel free, both to take time to explore what may be a new approach and to depart from the guidelines given here. Guidelines need to be departed from, and will be, by each of us, as we get caught up in the process of composing for the pulpit. Composing is a dynamic event and sometimes things happen in the course of it that have their own internal logic or rationale.

What we lack in homiletics as a discipline is a grammar, a way of talking about what we do that crosses over differences in theology or style. We have not yet identified basic rules that tend to operate in all good preaching, perhaps because we are not yet sure that they exist. A portion of what I will be saying will point to what I consider to be some universal principles that might begin to constitute a grammar of preaching. A grammar merely describes how patterns of meaning are generated within the given language structures according to predictable rules. When the rules are not observed, there may follow a breakdown of communication. But the subject of a possible grammar of preaching is necessarily the task of many people working together in a concentrated way and is beyond our scope here. Most of what will be found in these pages may be kept in mind simply as worthy goals in the service of proclaiming God's restorative Word to a hungry world.

CHAPTER TWO

The Biblical Text and Our Situation

Preparing to preach a biblical text should be like hearing the sound of a distant flute on the evening breeze. We strain to hear it, tilt toward it, are intrigued by it, and caught up in the sweetness of its sound. Here is music where there had been silence, music that we will carry with us through the week and will keep on experiencing in our hearts through the hospital visits and the meetings. The music comes to us like a tune we had forgotten, restoring the soul. It originated, of course, thousands of years ago, in the witness to God's salvation recorded by the ancient writers.

We begin listening to the biblical text on Monday. While today may be set aside mainly for rest and relaxation, the imagination of the heart needs mulling and brooding time. Said another way, today we begin our task as theologians for we begin to consider what David Tracy calls "the two principle sources for theology [which] are Christian texts and common human experience and language."[1] Imagination of the heart we have defined as imagination leavened by both scripture and experience; it regards Christ both in the brokenness of the world and in our dreams of a new order and relationship already transfigured by God's love, a new order which keeps breaking in each moment. Understanding that imagination may be assisted with basic skills, learned one step at a time, we will start in this chapter by developing the first steps of dealing with the biblical text and our situation.

Some of what I will be identifying are steps that imaginative preachers and careful listeners may already do intuitively but may not know they do. The process for them is still largely subconscious. The principles involved, however, are universal and function in all creative biblical preaching, even though for most preachers these principles are subconscious. Most of us do not have the skill or control of imagination that we could have to produce powerful sermons or homilies. Identifying the creative process for preaching can give us that control.

In the first chapter we began to look at imagination as the product of juxtaposition of opposites. We looked at opposites within the origin of some words and at juxtapositions created by reaching outside of individual words for a fresh opposite. Here I will try to open new ground in preaching by focusing primarily on how simple juxtaposition of groups of words, short phrases, and sentences—some from the biblical text and some from our own situation—can have powerful effect in making our preaching spark. Too often in books on preaching, old and familiar material is faithfully warmed up in the hope that new appreciation will be found. A long-standing problem that any amount of re-heating has failed to resolve is that once the exegesis is done we are not given detailed help with the biblical text that is set before us. Just when we may hope we will get specific suggestions on how to proceed, the writers often generalize, leaving us frustrated and discouraged. Here detailed assistance will be given to show exactly how a biblical sermon or homily can begin to write itself. As in the theory for any art, whether it be music, dance, or the homiletical art of imagination, much of the work is technical, requiring technical language which in part we will have to develop.

There has been much discussion in homiletics as to where one starts in preparing to preach. Here I will assume that the starting point generally is with the biblical text and with the biblical text alone. The particular needs of the congregation—always present in the preacher's mind and heart—are initially, intentionally, and temporarily kept at bay. If there is a pre-determined theme or special occasion such as an anniversary or baptism, this too will be kept at bay for now. The time for the encounter will come later.

The biblical text has not always been regarded as the starting point. Sometimes it has been said that a contemporary situation may be the begin-

ning. And far too often, no attempt is made to keep
the biblical text and our situation separate. This
can lead to problems, such as when the preaching
seems to be a lecture on the biblical text and the
congregation is left puzzled about connections
with their own lives. Biblical exegesis is not
biblical preaching. Or alternately we may discuss
the issues of the day and leave our people to make
what connections they can with the biblical texts
that were read. Between these two extremes there
is a wide variety of more responsible positions (i.e.,
expounding the meaning of a scripture for today,
possibly verse by verse, preaching on Christian
doctrines, treating broad themes of the Bible).
Nonetheless, failure to keep biblical text and our
situation separate but in relationship to each other
causes problems. They may be solved if we trust
the text to be our starting place, simply putting on
hold any ideas we have prior to studying the text
and coming back to them later.

In our preaching we want to make explicit and
implicit connections between the biblical text
and ourselves. The final goal will be a balanced
dialogue between the biblical text (in its own
context) and us (in our situation). The biblical
text and our situation will function for us as two
poles or opposites which, properly juxtaposed
and properly balanced, produce a third identity
which is the spark of imagination of the heart.
This spark is the essential meaning of the sermon
or homily. It may be closely related to the heart of
God's Word for today, bearing in mind that the
words we speak as preachers are never identical
to the Word that God speaks through us.

To arrive at a place where imagination has

appropriate opposites to juxtapose, there are some very important steps to follow:

Selecting the Biblical Text

Many preachers may think that preaching an imaginative sermon or homily begins with choosing an imaginative biblical text, one that seems fresh and that is rarely preached. This is an unfortunate idea. Nearly every biblical passage, taken in context of the verses around it, is filled with wonderful ideas about God's salvation: the difficulty is in releasing them from the text. For imagination, the choice of any particular text is less important than what we do with that text.

Whether we choose the text from a lectionary or find one on our own that promises rich harvest for preaching may depend on our tradition. There are advantages to both approaches, although lately those concerning the lectionary have received most attention. These include: (a) wide exposure to a broad section of the Scriptures over the three-year cycle, a yearly progression through the life and ministry of Jesus and systematic treatment of individual books for series preaching, (b) ecumenical advantages such as a ministerial Bible study, opportunities for interchurch or interdenominational study groups, and availability of a wide range of educational and homiletical support resources, and (c) the possibility of easy coordination of education and worship in the church. Following the other tradition of choosing one's own texts there are these advantages: (a) texts may be chosen that present current problems for members of the congregation, (b) the pastor has greater freedom to run a series from week to week on one topic drawing from a variety of texts, and (c) there is the ease and opportunity of selecting a different text as the Spirit moves. There are disadvantages to both approaches as well: since with neither will we cover the entire Bible, with each we could create a sub-canon of scripture within scripture.

Irrespective of which approach (or combination of approaches) to choosing scripture is followed, imagination of the heart demands that the text be allowed to stand on its own with the message of the entire sermon or homily arising from it and out of it, rather than being imposed on it. In addition, we want an entire section or pericope, not just one verse in isolation, as though the context of any verse is understood as irrelevant to its meaning.

Samuel Taylor Coleridge was one of the pioneers for us in seeing that each part of a written text related to the meaning of the whole and the whole affected the meaning of its parts. We want to hear what the Bible has to say to us, not what we have to say to the Bible. Furthermore, we should choose our text and stay with it. Sometimes we spend more energy and imagination *looking* for a text than we spend in *dealing* with the text we find. Most biblical texts have great potential for us.

Two assumptions about textual choice may seem new to many preachers:

1. *Any biblical text can speak to any contemporary situation.* This seems a ludicrous idea. Yet in a way it is what this book is about. Moreover, it may be one of the unconscious principles that governs those who preach from assigned texts.

None of us wants to run out of things to say, and each of us wakes up in the night pushing back the fear we might have nothing to offer. But if we learn to listen to each text, it will tell us what it says and how it addresses any particular situation.

There is an idea common among preachers that we are looking for a textual situation that might be the twin of our own situation. It has less truth in it than we might think. It can lead to predictable preaching: at a baptism we preach on Jesus' baptism; at a wedding we will read about the wedding at Cana; at a funeral we will speak about the house with many rooms; and at an anniversary we will recall the dedication of the Temple. There are some preachers, though they are unusual, who can take such predictable matching and produce from it a word that will lead people down new corridors in their lives. Most of us would produce preaching that is flat like a well-worn carpet, no longer noticed, except for wiping the feet as one passes. The reason is that there is very little spark, the poles are almost the same, and imagination has little room in which to move.

For powerful and imaginative preaching, the biblical text and our situation can be used as poles. Because God's Word is a living Word and speaks through every text, we are safe in assuming that when we bring an exegeted text into relationship with our situation, sparks are going to happen. We might try, to take an extreme example, preaching the marriage at Cana at a funeral, particularly since the wedding is almost incidental to the text, providing merely an occasion for celebration.

The most powerful biblical sermons and homilies are sometimes the ones that manage to make a simple and surprising connection we did not anticipate. We do not need to know what connections our imagination will make with our situation when we choose the scripture (although this may be frightening!). We will soon see how the connections can be created. This is part of the fun of preaching. We will find it doing to us what Ebeling and others suggested a text must do: it will interpret us.

2. *Choice of one primary text is helpful.* Roman Catholic and Protestant traditions have always assumed that every text read in worship need not be interpreted. A stronger statement may be needed, however: not every text read in worship *can* be treated in the sermon or homily, at least with the attention it deserves and we deserve. In the ten to twenty minutes most of us have available for preaching in worship, we want God's people to experience God's Word—that means choosing a primary text and giving more than just a sporting chance for its music to be heard. Moreover, in that time frame we are barely able to develop one text with biblical and historical integrity, much less two or three. Imagination flourishes best if the biblical channel is not being continually switched from one station to the next.

The normal goal might be to preach on one of the texts that we read in the service. By tradition this will be the Gospel yet frequently it may be the Old Testament or the Epistle. William Skudlarek advocates mentioning all lessons without forcing relationships. We might ask whether this meets

the preacher's need more than the congregation's:

> Thus, as you work with the gospel, and with the
> Old Testament lesson . . . keep your eye on the
> epistle. Let it be there, on the horizon, in the
> background, lurking, as it were, in the shad-
> ows. . . . Simply let yourself be open to the ways
> in which this lesson can draw further meaning
> from the text of the gospel, can throw light on
> it. . . . If you do this, you will, I believe, almost
> always be surprised and delighted by the unex-
> pected insights you receive.[2]

What he is talking about is, of course, what we
already recognize as the imagination functioning
to create a spark between two biblical texts that
are intentionally juxtaposed. For that matter, in
the preaching we might mention *any* biblical
story that would help bring the larger Christian
story into focus. Bringing texts alongside one
another can allow them to function as poles for
imagination. But I am convinced that if we do, the
sparks will be and need to be at superficial levels
of the texts, involving certain obvious images or
else resonant story lines (i.e., two texts might each
deal with a family dispute). These are appropriate
to our larger understanding of who we are as
God's people.

To attempt more than this important surface-
level sparking, however, will most likely result in
distorting the meaning of one or more of our texts.
The significance of this intertextual commuting
should not be overrated, however. *The spark that
we seek is not between biblical texts, it is between the
biblical text and our situation.* Preachers who have
a background in literary criticism have been

trained to do this kind of sparking between texts and may need to be intentional in re-routing their energies.

This choice of one primary text may guide even preachers using the lectionary, for which lessons were chosen with other lessons in mind.[3] Although this is the case, the passages were certainly not written, nor were they chosen, to say the same thing. Preaching cannot attempt to harmonize scripture lessons that are saying quite different things. For homiletical purposes our primary concentration needs simply to be on fully uncovering the light of one text for the darkness of today.

Imagining the Story of the Text

Most preachers were taught to rush immediately to the commentaries, as soon as a text was chosen. This can be a way of crippling the imagination. Our approach needs to be different, without displacing the importance of careful exegesis. Imagination needs room to move and opportunity to explore; it cannot be confined to the well-worn paths, even though it may continue to return to them. Checking the original Hebrew or Greek, if we have them, need not be delayed, for nuances of meaning in particular words and phrases may open fresh understanding for us. But before we turn to the familiar commentaries, before we try to remember relevant books or how we preached this text last time, before we begin even to think about what it means or to what doctrines it might relate, we may try to recapture some of the vitality of the text simply through imagining the story. When I ask groups to tell me the story of a text, I continue to be surprised how many people immediately start telling me its *meaning*. Enter the text and get caught up in it: recite its events, say what it says.

In imagining the story, we want to respond to the biblical text first of all in the brokenness of our humanity, with all of what we normally call our subjective responses, and then move to more informed stances. We are not just after a cerebral encounter with the text. It is the imagination of the heart we are after, with all of the Old Testament implications of the word heart. That we may decide that some of these responses are inappropriate, in light of our subsequent study, need not concern us now. We are wanting to stretch and loosen the text so that we may see it with fresh eyes.

It is not that we can have ready and immediate access to the hearts of the witnesses and to their stories even with knowledge of the period. However, as James Breech, the parables scholar, notes in summarizing the contribution of Amos Wilder, between the biblical time and our own, there is some "permanence in human nature and the nature of society. . . . There is some stability in the human psyche. . . . And the stable form of our human constitution guarantees some continuity in spite of the cultural differences."[4] Studies of New Testament texts, both Breech and Amos Wilder suggest, should lead us "to understand language in all of its dimensions—personal, historical, and social" and this Breech identifies as understanding "the operations of the imagination and the heart."[5] Neither Breech nor Amos

Wilder suggests that this continuity of experience can be obtained separate from scholarly endeavor. I suggest here, however, that continuity of experience *begins* in treating the text as a story. It is an experience that should start prior to, necessarily lead toward, and should continue throughout exegetical study.

The importance of imagining the story of a text, for purposes of imagination of the heart, stems from understanding contemporary art. Thomas H. Troeger, like many of us who studied English literature at university, heard his teacher warn against ever reading a critic on a poem before first of all reading and living with the text for yourself. "Otherwise," says Troeger, "we would rob ourselves of a raw encounter with the work."[6] Eugene Lowry, in analyzing the creative process in art, also points to the need to stay with the biblical text at a basic level, "not until something is solved but until something clearly is most *un*solved," at which point, he suggests, we should leave the creative process, do something completely different, and allow what he calls the "preconscious" to begin to work.[7] We may interpret him to be speaking of creating space for imagination to work. Some of what Walter Wink discusses in his *Transforming Bible Study* (Abingdon Press, 1980) may also be understood as getting at the story level of the biblical text, although he does not then connect this with serious exegesis.

Imagining the text as story is something we all probably do; we just do not pause long enough on it for it to become conscious and begin using it as a tool for imagination of the heart. The reason this step is important is that story is an art form that operates by its own rules. We may learn something from studying the story. In fact, Fred Craddock suggests that "the short story is a first cousin of the sermon." He also says that we should regularly read novels, short stories, and poetry—"at least one a week." His reasoning is as follows:

> Reading good literature enlarges one's capacities as a creative human being and has a cumulative effect on one's vocabulary, use of the language, and powers of imagination. Not by conscious imitation but through the subtle influence of these great storytellers and poets, a preacher becomes more adept at arranging the materials of the sermon so that by restraint and thematic control, interest, clarity, and persuasiveness will be served.[8]

By the same reasoning, we could say that attention to the story form in general expands our ability to experience the story of a biblical text.

Listening to a text sometimes is not enough— like Ezekiel in the mountain gaps we need to know for what we are listening. We want to be putting our ears to a chosen text, straining to hear through the words on the page the sounds that are there: perhaps the market buzz, or the family squabbles, the splash of well water being poured, the clank of the field hoe hitting a stone, hoofbeats in narrow lanes, the temple's echoing silence, or the baby's cry on the night breeze. These are, after all, the sounds of God's Word becoming flesh. We want to hear the text laughing and angry, we want to see where it pauses and where it rushes, we want to smell and taste the air it breathes, we want to touch what it touches. More than this, we want to respond to it, resist it, question it, enjoy it, be bothered by it. Our response does not have to be "nice." It should first of all be human. And this response may be most useful if it comes from our dark side. As Leander Keck says:

> Responses to this experienced intersection [of text and our time] frequently are not pious; they often include bafflement, irritation, or resistance. Instead of feeling guilty about them, one should recognize them as signs that an issue has been located that needs to be worked through, as symptoms that a word is being heard.[9]

This encounter with the text is like a new encounter with an old friend recently returned from the ancient Far East. The text already exists as story, with its own unity and life, and has more stories behind it. When we skip the story stage and rush to the exegesis, we put the fire extinguisher to imagination before it has had a chance even to spark.

But what if the text does not strike us as a story? What if we were dealing with Matthew's "woe to you" passage or one of Paul's instructions to the church in Corinth or an Old Testament law? Even here there is a story level of the text, it is just that many more of the story details are left out of the telling than in most Gospel stories. Every text has a story in it or behind it. We may not know many answers, but always know enough to ask questions. We follow the clues in the text. Paul and the Corinthians are juxtaposed. They are functioning like two "opposites." Insofar as Paul's letter is a kind of sermon, the poles are similar to the poles of biblical text (Paul's witness) and contemporary situation (the situation in Corinth). What are the sparks between them? We can be asking such questions as: Who are these people to whom Paul is writing? What are they doing? How does Paul know? What feeling is conveyed in these words? How would I feel if I were the one being addressed? Or if I were Paul?

We have been talking of imagination as the juxtaposition of opposites in language. This, we said, may result in what we normally think of as imagination—thinking in pictures. We do not want to be falling back to that simple under-standing here. Imagination in experiencing the story of the text certainly involves picturing the text, but it involves much more than this. It is a process involving the mind and all of the senses. Each of the senses has its own ways of triggering mental actions which might be the equivalent of pictures for the eye. Each of the senses contrib-utes to thoughts, feelings, and imagination. And each of the biblical texts was written for a variety of senses. Imagination is nurtured by our being sensitive to sensory and other clues imbedded in the text. The biblical writers used imagination: they juxtaposed certain words with others, certain images and sounds with other images and sounds. We seek to recover what sparks there were for the original writers.

We have little difficulty recognizing many of the Gospel accounts as story, if we set our hearts to it. But if we read Luke's story of Zacchaeus and decide what it *means* (for instance, that following Jesus demands repentance), we have missed the story. We may be partially right about the meaning, but the meaning is not a tooth to be yanked from an unexamined mouth. *Stories have many meanings.* And biblical texts have many correct meanings. We will decide later the meaning we want to develop as the product of exegesis and everything else. For now, just the story is the task. The story is what we should recite without looking at the text, trying to remember as many details as possible: "Jesus was in Jericho and there was a rich man, Zacchaeus, who wanted to see him, so Zacchaeus climbed a tree to see over the crowd."

Basic questions help us get behind the text to imagine the details not written but implied. These are the "who, where, what, why and when" questions, the "see, hear, smell, taste, and touch" questions, and the questions that identify our own emotional and intellectual response to the text. Thomas G. Long speaks of related categories when he speaks of the text's cognitive elements ("things we need to know"); emotional elements ("feelings we need to experience"), and behavioral elements ("actions we are called upon to perform").[10]

The kinds of questions we will ask about a biblical text will vary with the text. Consider the kinds of questions we might ask about the Zacchaeus story (Luke 19:1-10). They might be:

- What was special about Jericho as a city?
- What kind of day was it? What time? What season?
- What indicates Zacchaeus was rich?
- Did his clothes make him stand out from the rest?

- Why was there a crowd? Had it gathered for Jesus? Why?
- Even if Zacchaeus were short, why could he not see Jesus?
- Wouldn't the crowd let him through?
- Did they not tolerate him?
- If the crowd was pressing tightly around Jesus, why did it do that?
- Why did Zacchaeus want to see Jesus?
- Was it not unusual for a wealthy man to climb a tree?
- Did Jesus know Zacchaeus before? Is that why he calls him by name? Is this another instance of Jesus just knowing the stranger's name? Did he ask someone? Or were some jeering Zacchaeus and shouting his name? Might that be why Jesus picked him?
- Why did Zacchaeus repent? Did Jesus demand this? Or was it a free response to being recognized?
- Did Jesus give him stature that the job and the tree could not?
- Do I like the story? Who do I like? What do I dislike?
- When have I been like Zacchaeus? The crowd? Jesus?

Here are three general suggestions to help imagination of the heart get to its feet when we approach a text:

First, *it matters less what our questions are than that we now allow the questions to surface.* Questions free the imagination. Imagination requires a gap between the text and ourselves so there can be a spark. At this point in the preparation process (which we could also call the separation process, since we are eventually trying to separate what we think the text is saying because of our own contextual situations and what the text is actually saying in its own context), it does not matter that some of the questions we ask will not be answered either by the text or by our subsequent exegesis. Again, do not cut off the possibility of imagination before it has even had a chance. All *questions* of a text are valid; it is some of the *answers* that we might give that are not. Questions are like wild flowers bursting on the hillside, providing wonder and mystery, both of which are necessary for imagination.

Second, as in any education process, *the questions are more important than the answers.* If we have the questions we can always find the answers. But if we do not have the questions, any number of answers are as water on a duck's back. The questions allow the possibility of answers. They are essential preludes.

Third, *the "creative genius" is the one who asks questions about the smallest assumption.* Arthur Koestler's theory was that creative people refuse to be limited by the normative assumptions of their disciplines.[11] People who do not allow themselves to ask how Jesus knew Zacchaeus' name, or for whom it is obvious that Jesus demanded repentance of Zacchaeus (the text does not say this), have unknowingly trampled the flower of imagination.

In imagining the story it is often the "feeling" questions that are important. Some things in the text will stand out for you that will not stand out for me—this is one of the reasons that group Bible study is helpful for hearing the text afresh. Or again, we might follow the clues of our own minds and bodies: Why do I remember this and not that? When have I felt like that? With whom do I identify in the text? Why don't I identify with the others? What am I feeling right now? How old do I feel when I read this text? If the story of the text does not at first seem to have any preaching possibilities and seems uninteresting, it is the naming of these feelings that will often get us unstuck. Feelings are one form of bias, and identification of this bias is a helpful step in experiencing the text as story. Some of these feelings are responses to the text and elicited by the text and some have more to do with our own context as we read.

Of course as we are imagining the story we are also uncovering other biases we bring to the text besides feelings. Some are necessary to the interpretation process and some are unnecessary, and this can be determined both now and throughout the subsequent exegesis. Biases are political, economic, racial, educational, geo-graphical, sexual, cultural, religious—in short anything we can find to make us different from our brothers and sisters can work as a positive or negative bias. They can be some of the most helpful tools we have in subsequent exegesis.

Some excellent questions to identify these biases are: Do I like this text? Do I dislike it? Why? *Get to the place where the text begins either to excite you or to rub you the wrong way. This is the genuine starting place for preaching.* If a text bothers us, it is not that we will preach rejecting it or that we will hold it up to ridicule, for it is the Bible that in part is our authority to preach. Rather we will try to understand it in its own context, allowing our irritation with it to be a trustworthy guide in studying it. We bring our biases to the text in a conscious way and let them be addressed by our subsequent studies. Beginning to recognize our biases is part of being a responsible preacher. We can then determine whether or not they are appropriate and whether or not they will end up distorting the text. All of this is part of imagining the story of a text.

If imagining the story still sounds strange and foreign to you, try doing what should be done with stories: tell them. Tell the story of the text to parishioners you see during the week, or ask a garage attendant to listen for a minute, and listen to the reactions. Ask them to tell the story to you. Part of experiencing the text as a story is telling and retelling. In addition, *treat the text like a pair of eyeglasses*. Put on these glasses early in the week and view the entire events of the week through the lenses of the text. Parts of the story you had not noticed before will come alive for you. Never take off these glasses. Remind yourself that you have them on. This entire process is the true beginning of interpretation and imagination. We are encountering the text as though we are hearing it for the first time. We are discovering a strangeness of first experience which is an essential step in the homiletical process.

Guessing the Meaning

We may now ask ourselves about the text's specific *meaning*. At this stage it is still a hunch, a guess, an idea about what the text might mean. For instance, if we said of the Zacchaeus story that, "Following Jesus demands repentance," and this is what the text means to us at this stage, then this is what we are after. The fact that it might be wrong (as in this case it is—Zacchaeus' change is a free and natural response to an encounter with Jesus) does not reduce its value as a first guess. It could also prove to be right and may be a fresh angle that the biblical commentators have not covered. Keep it short, as short as possible. Write it down. It is where we are starting from and will later help plot the route we have taken. We all have a first guess about a text's meaning. Most of us simply do not take time to state it. It is one of the unconscious thoughts we all have in homiletics but generally do not name. The naming of it can give control and direction to the homiletical process. We are trying to make conscious the steps of homiletical preparation for the purpose of increasing our skill with imagination.

For Bultmann and others in the field of hermeneutics, the pre-understanding is the entire understanding we bring to bear on any text prior to fresh study. It is all of the baggage we take with us to the text. Our first guess has moved us somewhat beyond that pre-understanding, but it is not yet in the category of authentic meaning. It is a short sentence saying what we think is the essential meaning of the text. It reflects where we have been, the initial "strangeness" of the text. It also looks ahead carrying with it the question we will address to the text in our exegesis. "Could it be," we will be saying to the text through it, "that this is a fair statement of what you mean?"

In looking at the first guess, we are looking at what may eventually turn out to be the sermon or homily in embryonic form. It is not yet the theme or central idea. When we write it down it stands as a symbol of our encounter with the text as story which we would otherwise forget in doing exegesis. If we lose sight of what route we took to arrive at our understanding of a text, we will also be forgetting the level at which many of our people may be encountering the text when they hear it in worship. In our preaching they may need us to guide them from that place if they are to come to our new sense and appreciation of the text.

The Concerns of the Text

Let us imagine for a moment that we have already completed our exegesis. (Shortly I will return to discuss exegesis in detail.) It is done and we may have been walking about our own town with our exegesis in mind imagining the Zacchaeus story. We may have studied short and tall people on the street, or imagined Zacchaeus sitting up high, perhaps in the lifeguard's chair at the pool. We may have thought of the crowd of teenagers at the restaurant window as the citizens of Jericho looking in at Jesus who was eating with the sinner. Several possibilities that might otherwise have gone unnoticed in the text will have opened up to us. Now we can begin taking the steps that will allow ideas and images from the pole of the biblical text to spark with the pole of our situation. This process lies at the core of powerful and imaginative biblical preaching.

What follows in relation to concerns of the text
and later, to concerns of the sermon or concerns of
the homily, will be new for homiletics—new with
regard to the terminology and idea and new in
suggesting that this is how to allow our material
to catch fire with imagination. Again, however, it
will be something many of us may already do
unconsciously without naming it. As such it may
be one of the basic unacknowledged grammatical
rules that already functions in homiletics. Concerns of the text will set up a biblical "pole" for
imagination. Concerns of the sermon (or concerns
of the homily) will function as the "pole" of our
contemporary situation and time. The identification of these two will keep the biblical text and
our situation separate so that there can be
independence and a genuine juxtaposition and
creative sparking between opposites.

*A concern of text is each and every idea with
which a biblical text is legitimately concerned. It is a
short statement of that idea in sentence form,
expressing a complete thought.* It uses the exact
details of the text but does not generally use the
text's word order or sentences. Where necessary,
these are rephrased. Thus each and every concern
of the text is in fact an interpretation of the text. *It
may come directly from the text, it may be implied by
a textual detail, or it may come from supporting
exegetical material.* The first guess as to what the
text means will be one of these concerns of the text
if it has proven to be authentic.

Every intentional act of communication involves three actions: (1) reduction, (2) representation, and (3) expansion.

The first, reduction, is apparent, for instance, if

we are writing a letter; we obviously cannot write about everything. In fact, if we had to write about everything that happened to us in a five-minute interval, it might take us a whole day: we would have to write about all the sensations our body experienced, about the thoughts that drifted in and out of conscious thought, plus explanation about the place where we are, about the colors we saw, and on and on. Thus, when we communicate something that potentially could be described by an infinite number of words and combinations, we choose to *reduce* it to a few words.

The second action, representation, comes into play because we allow these few words to *represent* something about our original larger experience.

The third action, expansion, operates when we assume a commonality of experience with our reader. That person takes what we have said and *expands* it to create an experience similar to our own. If we were to represent the complex process of communication (reduction, representation, expansion) in the simplest way, the diagram might look like this:

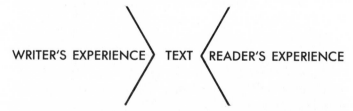

WRITER'S EXPERIENCE 〉 TEXT 〈 READER'S EXPERIENCE

Concerns of the text may be understood as part of an identical reduction-representation-expansion process. Where even the biblical writer reduced a broad experience to a few words, so too, we take these few words of the biblical text and reduce them to still fewer manageable words and ideas. These we then expand to form the sermon or homily.

BIBLICAL TEXT   CONCERN(S) OF THE TEXT   SERMON/ HOMILY

In the same way the congregation's role may be plotted, for the process of communication is a long series of reductions and expansions, of funneling in and funneling out.

PREACHER'S EXPERIENCE   SERMON/HOMILY   CONGREGATION'S EXPERIENCE

I am convinced that we all go through a mental process of writing concerns of the text even if this is unconscious: reduction and expansion is simply the way we come to understand. To make it conscious is to gain more control over communication and ensure faithfulness to the text. But the most important reason for identifying concerns of the text is that it is with these concerns that the text begins to work for us. *Many students in particular approach a biblical text for preaching with the misguided understanding that there is one correct interpretation of the text that they must find, and this single-minded search for one idea shuts down creativity.* Writing out the concerns of the text begins to show how vast are the potential preaching ideas in any text. If we know how to pull concerns of the text from the text, we need never fear running dry in preaching.

Let us try writing some concerns of the text now, starting with some nursery rhymes for which exegesis is largely impossible. The religious and emotional freight we often bring to biblical texts can prevent us from understanding what a concern of the text might be. We can avoid this problem by focusing for the moment on the concerns of the nursery rhyme "Jack Sprat":

> Fat did not agree with Jack.
> Lean did not agree with his wife.
> Jack was married.
> Jack ate with his wife.
> They lived together. (The text does not tell us this, but "exegesis" of origin and culture might suggest it.)
> Jack was thin and his wife was fat. (The text also does not say this, but we might hazard a safe guess, based on contemporary data.)
> They had (what we would consider) bad manners.

Among the things we could say of "Little Bo Peep" might be:

> She was not a good shepherd.
> She worried needlessly.
> Whoever is speaking knows better than she does. (All of this is based on the presumption that the "leave them alone" is not said by her, which is one decision we must make for ourselves and be able to justify as at least a plausible interpretation.)
> We might also say:

Her sheep are not stupid (even if this contra-
   dicts what we know of sheep) or
The person giving the advice is.

Of "Baa, Baa, Black Sheep" we could suggest:

The black sheep has wool.
The black sheep gives everything it has.
It is owned by a man and woman.
It talks. (And so on.)

A concern we might all suggest for "Humpty
Dumpty" is that he was an egg, but unless we
could determine the rhyme's origin, (for instance,
in "Ring Around a Rosie" the origin lay in the
pockmarks of the smallpox plague) we would not
be justified. The text (or history) must give us
specific evidence of this.

So much for nursery rhymes. Biblical texts, as
texts, are essentially no different, except that we
have exegetical detail to draw on as well for the
concerns of the text. Any detail, like a scratch on a
new car or a flea on a dog's back, can be a concern.
The concerns of the text for Zacchaeus will consist
of earlier ideas from imagining the story, as well
as new ideas that will come from exegesis. Many
will be found in the short sentences of what we
will call a thumbnail exegesis. Remember to keep
the sentences here short. Omit unnecessary
adjectives or qualifying phrases (you can add
necessary qualifications when you *expand* these
concerns in the sermon or homily itself). If you
have a compound sentence, divide it. My list of
the concerns of this text is long but includes:

Zacchaeus was short. (This by tradition—the text's grammar is unclear, and the early church debated whether it was Jesus or Zacchaeus who was small.)

Zacchaeus is a publican and the chief tax collector.

He is open to charges of being doubly corrupt.

He is rich.

"Zacchaeus" means "righteous."

Jericho is a rich trade-route city.

Jesus is passing through.

Jesus invited himself to dinner.

Eating with sinners broke with Pharisaic law.

Jesus' love departs from wisdom.

He was compelled to stay with Zacchaeus. ("I must stay.")

Zacchaeus is surprised.

He welcomes Jesus with joy.

The crowd is surprised.

Zacchaeus is a sinner.

Jesus makes no demands.

Zacchaeus responds in repentance.

Zacchaeus' restitution for defrauding exceeds the OT law (Lev. 6:5; Num. 5:7).

Zacchaeus demonstrates a new attitude toward wealth.

Zacchaeus' repentance bears fruit.

Salvation for Zacchaeus comes in opening his heart to the poor and the cheated.

The sentences are short and simple and they correspond to the specific details of the text or exegesis. Each sentence from the biblical text might yield several concerns of the text. For instance, Luke 19:4 reads: "So he ran ahead and climbed a sycamore-fig tree to see him, since Jesus was coming that way." From this we could get the following concerns of the text (and we get more by consulting the commentaries for relevant background information): Zacchaeus ran ahead; he climbed a tree; he wanted to see Jesus; he knew which way Jesus was going; Jesus was coming. It may seem hard at first but try it. With time you find that it is a very simple but important and overlooked exercise. *The effect of concerns of the text is to dislodge ideas from the text in order that they may be heard anew or for the first time.* This is genuine "overhearing" of the gospel. The text is now broken down or reduced into manageable units with which imagination can work.

Exegesis

I have allowed us to jump ahead. We have discussed concerns of the text before we have discussed the exegesis *which should precede them.* The reason is this: in doing exegesis for preaching, it is the concerns of the text, and the data that supports them, for which we are looking. Our normal movement in homiletics may be from imagining the story, to guessing its meaning, to exegesis, to the concerns of the text. We are tilting toward the past as we listen to the biblical text and it is our exegesis that keeps us from losing our balance and falling flat on our face.

How do we do exegesis in a way that will assist the imagination? The first thing we may keep in mind is that every biblical text has a variety of possible correct interpretations; there is never just one. Around every text there is what we may think of as an invisible circle. This *arena of authentic interpretation* contains all the valid concerns of any text. We can never actually define where the boundary line for this arena exists, but we know it is there because some interpretations are wrong and clearly lie outside it. For instance, the meaning of the Zacchaeus story is clearly not that short people make good. The ideas that arise from our earlier imagining the story of any particular text must be verified; they must be proven to be within this arena of authentic interpretation. We verify concerns of the text through exegesis.

Every textbook on preaching should say something about exegesis, although not all do. Here I want to be as brief as possible, stating some basic presuppositions and concentrating only on those aspects of exegesis for preaching that are too often overlooked.

It is a fairly recent suggestion in homiletics that we approach exegesis with an already well-established sense of the text. Quite the contrary has sometimes been true: preachers who have had a strong sense of the text have often assumed that exegesis was unnecessary. When we give in to this temptation we are not trusting God's Word to be a living Word that will speak to us in fresh ways today if we will only stay with it long enough.

To this point we have been stretching the text and loosening its parts in order that imagination may have room to move. We want to keep on being imaginative as we turn to study the text in a scholarly way. We continue the activity already begun concerning the text and ourselves, allowing ourselves to be irritated, prodded, bored, or excited. Martin Marty says that what makes a sermon good is "creative listening,"[12] which may be similar to Bonhoeffer's idea of listening with expectation of encountering the risen Christ or similar again to what Leander E. Keck calls "priestly listening."[13] Now we extend that "creative listening" not just to the biblical text but also to the commentators. As a colleague of mine once said, "We should read the commentators expecting to find water, even though the pages may be as dry as dust." The biblical commentators, far from being roadblocks to us as we move down the road to preaching, are instead like the tourist information booths that guide us in the right direction, pointing out the things we should see and preventing us from getting lost.

There are three categories of basic biblical material we are after: the circumstances that led to a text being written; the culture in which it was written, including dominant cultural ideas and norms; and the writer's personal theology or world-view.[14] When we talk about the biblical text in its own culture, it is the identification of these elements to which we are referring: we are what Barth called "the witnesses of the second order," seeking the spark that the events described in the text had for "the witnesses of the first order." This is the whole purpose of exegesis. As Keck says, "The exegetical process . . . is not complete until the text is released into the present-day form of that community for which it was written in the first place."[15] This can stand as a definition of biblical preaching.

Imagination of the heart cannot exist without

the Scriptures: it is imagination informed by both
scripture and experience. The role of the Holy
Spirit in this is to be recognized. I recall seeing a
sign for a Bible study group in a student lounge. It
said: "Leave your commentaries at home—it is
just us and the Holy Spirit." The assumption can
be all too common, that the Holy Spirit does not
use scholarship, even as other students might
question the role of prayer in studying a text.
Martin Marty reminds us that all human creativity has God as its source. He calls prayer "a great
underutilized form in connection with creativity. We usually think of prayer as a set-aside time,
routinized or panic time, but if it is true that
human creativity is involved in divine creativity
there is no way to get there except prayer."[16]
Prayer can be a guide to us throughout the
homiletical task as the Roman Catholic practice
of "praying a text" can testify.

When we have finally determined, with the help
of commentaries and prayer, the meaning of a
text we will preach, we still acknowledge that
there are many other possible meanings, many
more things to be said. This is true even of
parables, which have often been said to make only
one point; as I tell my students, scholars have
never been able to agree on which point they
make. As Helmut Gollwitzer has noted, we always
will "leave [the text] the freedom to speak to
others in a manner different from the way it
speaks to us, and [we will] . . . leave others the
freedom to find other things than we have
succeeded in finding."[17]

Let us move on to some new or too-often-over-
looked suggestions for exegesis that can assist us.

Things to do in exegesis:

1. *Try to prove wrong the first guess at the text's meaning.* Instead of setting out to prove we are right (which, if we are determined, is often too easy to do at the expense of the truth), this goal in exegesis sets us out under the judgment of the text.

2. *Put all thoughts of our own time and situation out of our minds, as much as this is possible, including thoughts of the people to whom we will be preaching.* If we do not, they will talk to us as we are trying to concentrate on what the biblical writers and their commentators are saying. There will be plenty of time to talk with them later.

3. *Write a thumbnail exegesis.* This is a concise survey (less than a page in length) of the most useful related exegetical material. *It is essentially a collection of concerns of the text.* Data that will be useful to support any of these concerns as they will be developed in the preaching needs to be remembered but not recorded. The purpose is to have the essential meanings you will work with laid out in front of you for quick reference. The exercise can be done quickly and should include only material that might be useful for you in preaching. Keep the sentences short.

4. *Use good commentaries.* Most of the one-volume or old Bible commentaries are not worth the time it takes to find gems in them. Even *The Jerome Biblical Commentary,* recent though it is, is too brief for preachers. If a commentary does not back up what it says with data that we can examine, it should be discarded. We need to be able to support what we say if we are asked. A commentator saying, "Jesus meant this . . . ," is no proof; supporting something generally means

providing two or three separate pieces of evidence. Speculation is still speculation, whether it
is found in a commentary or anywhere else.
Undue reverence for commentators is crippling
for preaching. Where they disagree, we might
offer our own suggestions.

5. *Use suspicion in reading.* This does not
mean that we mistrust the Bible. Quite the
opposite is true. But we are reluctant to trust
what anyone says about it in case the Bible is
being distorted. Question the text and question
the commentators.[18]

6. *Use contemporary criticism to provide choices
for you and your people with the biblical text.* Our
task is to offer our people some of the choices that
are made available to us through our studies and
the studies of great Christian scholars, so they
may make mature faith-decisions for themselves
at their basic level of textual encounter. It is a sad
fact that modern biblical study is referred to as
"the best-kept secret of the church," given that
many graduates of seminaries recognize that
their own faith has been strengthened by it.

7. *Recognize that every text has many layers.* For
instance, in preaching on a parable we might
choose to preach on what might have been Jesus'
original version, or on the version recorded for
instance by Matthew, or on the interpretation
Matthew adds to the parable. Normally we would
choose one. In a properly exegeted text, there are
many options open to us.

8. *Guard the text's integrity.* If we do not make
clear in the sermon or homily what is in the text
and what is not, we can create difficulties. If our
people go to the text after the service (as we hope

they will want to do) thinking it says one thing when it says another, they may either not trust themselves as suitable readers of the Bible or they may not trust us to interpret it for them.

Things to avoid in exegesis:

1. *Do not psychologize the text.* This means we avoid false creativity, creativity that does not lead us to the heart of the text. Psychologizing is attributing psychological motivation to a character in a biblical story, for instance when we suggest that the prodigal son was unstable, when in fact the texts and their historical background are not interested in motive. There is a fine line here between psychologizing and authentic interpretation, and each of us must be our own judge. If we say that Zacchaeus lacked emotional stature and can back it up with details of the text (the crowd disliked him; he was surprised at Jesus' invitation; he repented when Jesus gave him identity) then it is not psychologizing. A good rule to follow if we are tempted to psychologize the text is to *psychologize us instead.* The text will not be distorted. Say, for example, "How would we feel in a situation like this?" We are not then saying that the text says what it does not say.

2. *Do not seek to explain or moralize the text.* This is a tough issue because, as with so many things in life, the preachers who moralize do not think that they do it. Moralizing allows no room for imagination. We do not want to turn the text into our own set of rules by which to live. Nor do we want to "explain away" the material, allowing our own cultural biases to justify what we would have said anyway, with or without the text. What others have said will help clarify this issue:

Moralism holds up the virtues, be they yesterday's piety, courtesy, and cleanliness, or today's
openness, frankness, and freedom, and makes a
deadly transposition. Instead of offering its list of
virtues as possible goals or consequences of the
gospel, moralism subtly *prescribes* them as the
means by which the grace of God is appre-
hended . . . at least half the sermons I read are
moralistic. These sermons usually preach Jesus-
our-example and think that by mentioning his
good behavior they have preached the gospel . . .
[which cannot be the case since] the congregation
is . . . thrown back upon its own powers of
imitation.[19]

[With moralizing, the biblical text] simply serves
as a catalyst; the actual content of the sermon is
derived elsewhere and frequently could have
been suggested just as well by a fortune
cookie. . . . The parable of the prodigal son
produced sermons on the importance of self-
discovery, which were triggered by the line,
"when he came to himself . . . "! Such a
sermon . . . does not make the text relevant, but
actually makes it irrelevant.[20]

Propositional and moralistic sermons both have
one fault in common: They fail to mediate the
actions of a saving Lord, because they fail to
allow us to experience those actions for ourselves.
They tell us about them; they never let us enter
into them in the imaginations of our hearts.[21]

Instead of moralizing, we will want to open up
responsible faith choices to our people and invite
them into the mystery of the faith. This does not
preclude, however, that there is a form of

legitimate moral instruction that arises out of many texts and is entirely appropriate for our purposes. Perhaps we need to make a distinction between moral content that properly arises out of the text and that which is imposed upon the text from our own cultural norms.

3. *Do not accept what commentaries say is the relevance for today.* These are and can only be suggestions. It is you, the preacher working in the daily life of the congregation, who knows your congregation better than anyone and knows the importance of the text in your parish. The best commentaries available today are tentative about how the text should be treated by the preacher: Eduard Schweizer's commentaries on Matthew (1975), Mark (1970) and Luke (1984) are models of what commentaries should be, while *The Interpreter's Bible* on Luke stands in the opposite extreme.

The Concerns of the Sermon
(The Concerns of the Homily)

The process of identifying concerns of the sermon/homily is essential for imagination in preaching. From the beginning I have suggested keeping our situation (the congregation and contexts to which we will preach) away, like a hound at bay. Now, as we loosen the leash, we will begin to experience the excitement of this approach. The concerns of the text form one set of poles or opposites and the concerns of the sermon/homily form another. We defined a concern of the text as each and every idea with which a biblical text is legitimately concerned. *A concern of the sermon (concern of the homily) may be defined as*

*a transposed version of a concern of the text,
generalizing the textual details in order to speak to
our situation. The concern of the text deals with the
text in its time; the concern of the sermon/homily
deals with our situation.* The concern of the text
deals with the past; the concern of the sermon/
homily deals with the present. Every concern of
the text has a concern of the sermon/homily.

In music, transposing involves writing or
playing in a different key from the one designated
by the musical score. Here, we are similarly after
a change in key: the connection of the original (the
concern of the text) with the transposed version
(the concern of the sermon/homily) cannot be lost.
The tune must be the same since the concern of
the sermon/homily can only derive its authority
from the text.

Although we are still early in the homiletical
process (even as we are early in the week) we may
anticipate that *the situations in our world to
address arise out of the text itself.* This does not
mean that the text limits the possible situations
we might address. The opposite is true. The text
discloses the limitless possibilities available to us
and suggests how the connections can be made.
As we juxtapose concerns of the text with
concerns of the sermon/homily, and as we
experience the sparks, we may glimpse how a
sermon or homily might begin to write itself:

1. Transposing Law

Abbreviations: **T** = concern of the text; **S** = concern
of the sermon/homily

T: Zacchaeus was short.
S: We lack stature; or, we often are unrecog-
          nized; or, our poor are unseen.

T: Jericho is a rich trade-route city.
S: Our cities are rich.

T: Jesus is passing through Jericho.
S: Jesus is passing through our town.

T: Jesus invites himself to dinner.
S: Jesus invites himself to stay with us.

T: Jesus is compelled to stay with Zacchaeus.
S: Jesus cannot stay away from the sinner.

T: Zacchaeus is surprised by Jesus' action.
S: We are surprised by Jesus.

T: Zacchaeus welcomes Jesus with joy.
S: We welcome Jesus with joy; or, The sinner knows how to welcome Jesus.

T: The crowd is surprised.
S: The righteous are surprised by Jesus.

T: Jesus makes no demands.
S: Jesus' love is a gift.

T: Zacchaeus responds to love with repentance.
S: Grace precedes repentance.

T: Opening his heart to the poor comes with his salvation.
S: Opening to the needs of the poor (or, wronged) comes with our salvation.

To arrive at these transpositions a simple procedure is to circle or highlight the individual words (or word groupings) in the concerns of the text and to find a substitute or synonym for each one. For instance:

Jesus	is compelled	to stay with	Zacchaeus.
Jesus	must	to dwell	us
God	cannot help but	to rest	sinner
The church		be with	outcast
			one of low stature

The process is one of free-association. It is identical to what we did with individual words in the last chapter in dealing with "salvation" and "eating a meal." Just do one word at a time and see what comes up. This can be and should be a very playful act. Then read over the possible sentences for concerns of the sermon/homily which, if elaborated, we could affirm in faith.

As soon as the poles or opposites are juxtaposed, sparks begin to fly for us. Every powerful biblical sermon or homily we have ever heard has involved this kind of relationship between a concern of the text and a concern of the sermon/homily, even though these names have not have been used and we may not have been able to name what was so powerful. This is another one of the universal yet unwritten grammatical rules of homiletics.[22] If we see how it is done, we can do it ourselves. The concerns of the text stay true to the details of the text: if the text said "disciples" then the concern of the text would say "disciples," and only in the concern of the sermon/homily would we find *we* or some other element of modern life and our situation. What we are doing, in effect, is moving the ideas through a time-change. To maintain the resonance between the two, some of the words often remain intact. We never want to lose continuity with the concern of the text, for it is the biblical

text that gives us our authority to preach.
Concerns of the text and concerns of the sermon/
homily are our aim, but do not be afraid to try or
to make mistakes. This need not be a solitary
exercise. We can try these exercises with friends
and colleagues.

Much preaching that is flat and lacking sparks
of creativity, fails because it does not establish the
polarity between text and our time. The two
become blurred: either the congregation is not
sure if the preacher thinks they are living two
thousand years ago or else Jesus seems so trendy
the congregation wonders why they need the
Bible.

Scripture is filled with exciting ideas and
events and imagination creates additional ones.
You may not agree with all of the transpositions
that I have made; you will want to try some for
yourself. At this stage in the homiletical process
we do not have to agree even with each one of our
own. As when juxtaposing individual words, we
do not cut short the creative process by instant
rejection. Allow imagination the time to explore
the tensions between concerns of the text and
concerns of the sermon/homily. We cut short
creativity by immediately deciding that a transposition is wrong before we have even bothered to
jot it down or to think it through.

Metaphors, as we said earlier, have both a yes
and no about them. The short sentences of the
concerns cannot hope to capture the whole truth
in themselves. They are rather like makeshift
taxis that can help ferry us to where we need to go.
It will be in the sermon or homily itself that we
will provide the necessary qualifications and

supportive data. In fact, the greater the distance between the two poles (provided that there is still a spark, still a relationship between the two to be made) the more this juxtaposition will both give us and demand us to say in the sermon or homily in order to make the connections clear for our people. The preaching will to some extent be the sum of the sparks that span the gaps between the concerns of the text and the concerns of the sermon/homily. Our work in keeping text and our situation separate has made this possible.

How many of these juxtapositions of text and situation we would use in one sermon or homily, how we would organize them, and how we would develop them will vary. These are subjects to be addressed in the next chapters when we will introduce further sparks to our process. In this chapter we have focused on the tasks for Monday. We have chosen the biblical text, imagined the story of the text, made a guess at the text's meaning, developed and verified through exegesis some concerns of the text, and finally we have moved to concerns of the sermon/homily. Although we have taken considerable time to go through these steps in detail here, the actual doing of them, from start to finish, need only take one or two hours. While the ideas presented here may sound difficult to practice, they are in fact very simple once understood. Having started so early in the week we will be giving imagination of the heart plenty of time to deepen our understanding of the sparks we have created. The first stage of preparation for preaching is now complete.

CHAPTER THREE

Law and Gospel/ Judgment and Grace

It is tough to be a preacher and pastor. However excited we may feel about our work, when discouragement comes we are still expected to stand up and preach encouragement to the congregation. In such circumstances doing what young John Wesley was told to do when he was experiencing a crisis of faith may be of some help: "Preach faith till you have it; and then, because you have it, you will preach faith." The advice is sound, whether or not we feel as windblown as Wesley. But more detailed guidelines would be helpful. How do we preach faith?

Paul said that "we preach Christ crucified" (I Cor. 1:23), but that is not enough. We understand from Paul's wider writing and his understanding of resurrection that we preach Christ crucified and risen. Here we have the seed for what Gerhard Ebeling said was "the basic guiding principle of theological thought and therefore as the decisive standard of theological judgement."[1] Preaching faith means measuring everything we preach by crucifixion and resurrection, in other words, by the categories of judgment and grace or law and gospel.

The concepts of judgment and grace or law and gospel are well-established within systematic theology and are well-known especially within classic Lutheran homiletics. Many of the problems that have beset the law-gospel distinction in systematics have dogged homileticians interested in adapting these terms to speak about the structure of preaching.[2] Law and gospel at best remain general tools for preaching, the most frequent recommendation being, as Herman Stuempfle made in his *Preaching Law and Gospel*[3] that our preaching should contain both law and gospel, since this is the nature of God's Word. There has been a general suggestion in systematics, variously attributed to Paul, Augustine, the early Luther, and others, that the proper sequence is law-gospel. But while this has had much traditional support, it has also been attacked for a variety of reasons. For instance, Karl Barth's 1935 essay "Gospel and Law" reversed the sequence to gospel-law-gospel to emphasize that law arises out of the gospel. The effect of all of this for preaching has been to neutralize anything but general homiletical possibilities for these terms.

Until now the terms law and gospel or judgment and grace have been explored and argued, but never fully combined with a homiletical approach. All of this might seem to recommend that the terms be dropped in favor of pursuing less contentious categories for homiletics. If other categories were readily available this would be an attractive option, but they are not. Part of the purpose of preaching, as we have been defining it, has been the recovery and restoration of the words of our faith for our people. Perhaps here our goal can be to attempt to give these words practical homiletical significance for the preacher. What we will be trying to do in this chapter is to turn these general ideas into specific tools for imagination of the heart.

The benefits of our attempt may outweigh the obvious risks. First, we will see in detail how to arrive at what will be the central idea of the sermon or homily. We already noted that as preachers we may often be frustrated by books on preaching which generally are vague precisely at the points where we need them to be specific. How we arrive at the central idea is one case in point. Second, these tools will create a spark between two broad and key theological ideas that will give thrust and direction to our preaching. Understanding the juxtaposition of law and gospel or judgment and grace can be one of the most helpful steps we can take in releasing imagination. Without it, even the most exciting sparks between biblical text and our situation can end up being smothered. Third, we will wed these ideas to the concerns of text and concerns of sermon/homily we have been developing. We will emerge with detailed guidelines as to how the biblical text may instruct our preparations.

Preachers often wish their preaching could be

more effective. By the time the heat of the day is upon the city, or later still, when the cold of the night has slipped into the valley, the "if only" chorus has been sung many times: "If only these youths could know God's love, or if only this old woman, or this mother in distress, or this unemployed man—if only they could know, would it not make the difference for which they long?" The times when we have even sung it for ourselves include when our attempts to proclaim the faith have seemed forced, when our words sounded to us as predictable as the news reports rattling in the background, and when the pain of the world has come too close.

One way for most preachers to become more effective is to lean more into the future, to claim Christ's future promise as it meets us in the present. This is the hope that pacifies the lion and encourages the lamb; that consoles the unconsolable; that comforts the uncomfortable; that reconciles the irreconcilable; that binds the exile in a foreign land to the sweet abundance of homecoming; that finds wholeness through brokenness; that offers forgiveness where there are debts; that proclaims life where there is death; and that makes inseparable the cry of dereliction on the cross from the hushed joyous resurrection utterance of Mary's "Rabboni!" Over and over again we have seen God's Word overturning the way of the world in our lives, yet too often in our preaching we stand upright, failing to lean into the future to claim the grace that is already ours.

Many of us may not understand the differences implied in Paul's use of law and gospel, judgment and grace. They are difficult ideas made more difficult by the fact that absolute distinction between them in practice is not possible. We cannot divide God's Word into the words of law and the words of gospel for this Word is one and the same. It is this idea, perhaps more than any other, that stands in the way of homiletical method. John Calvin in his *Institutes of the Christian Religion* says that law has a twofold movement toward judgment and grace. The same argument may be made about gospel. Judgment and grace are involved in both law and gospel. The Word that condemns may be the same word that saves. It is the Holy Spirit alone who can make the distinction. And this is precisely the impasse against which we always come in trying to adopt the terms for homiletics.

It will be helpful to keep in mind that our task in preaching is not to make final distinction between the two so much as it is to provide structures that will enable each to be heard. Many political meetings are structured to minimize the voices of opposition. Similarly many sermons or homilies, often through neglect or ignorance, are structured such that the complementarity of God's Word is denied. The issue may be illustrated at the most rudimentary level. If the preaching is angry, tender messages of love imbedded in it may never be heard. Sermons and homilies can be structured such that words of comfort (or, alternatively, words of reproach), may be uttered but never heard or received.

Although we cannot determine whether God's Word will strike us as demand or promise, condemnation or confirmation, we can try to ensure that the necessary elements are in place in our preaching that are most likely to enable the reception of God's Word as both law and gospel or judgment and grace. Homiletical structure is not something that just happens over which we have neither control nor responsibility. If structures are not present to bear law or gospel, judgment or grace, then we are accountable. We cannot feign innocence, impotence, or lack of fertility. We may understand law and gospel as two different *functions*, two different *actions*, two different *receptions*, or two different *ways in which we experience* God's Word. These modes may be anticipated, provided for, and encouraged. When we preach we offer ourselves as vehicles for God to use; similarly when we preach we may offer structures within the preaching that God may use. This cannot mean that the Holy Spirit necessarily will choose to use our offering as we anticipate. But it does mean that as preachers we cannot afford the luxury of avoiding what these terms mean to practice. To ignore them we may inadvertently end up preaching either law or gospel divorced from each other, which then can be self-serving and self-justifying philosophy, not God's Word.

Most preaching in every denomination fails to have structures in place that will enable law and gospel. The result is one of the chronic problems of our age—preaching that lacks good news. Since structures for law and gospel or judgment and grace are not established as poles or opposites, the effect can be to shrink the meaning of our message and to narrow its possible relevance. God's Word is spacious. The word salvation in Hebrew means "wide open spaces." God's Word frees the heart and loosens faith and imagination. As Jesus said, it is a Word whose burden is light. Why is it that we have such difficulty sharing with God the responsibility for a proclaimed word whose burden is light?

In this chapter I develop the structures that will help bear out this truth, that God's Word overturns the world. The structures suggested here may be only one way to achieve what we are after, but it is a way that can be effective. I will be supporting what others have said that law and gospel should both be present in preaching. But I will also be showing how to develop basic skills that can enable us to find potential law and gospel in a variety of ways in each biblical text. And further, I will be arguing that preaching, generally speaking, will move structurally from judgment to grace, or from law to gospel, and that a balance between the two will be sought. In turning law and gospel into specific tools for imaginative preaching, readers may remember that suggestions as to what is law or gospel in any specific text cannot be definitive since this is not in our control. Our efforts are best understood as attempts to identify language structures that are most likely to be capable of bearing law or gospel.

What the Terms Mean

There are sufficient readers for whom the terms law and gospel or judgment and grace are unclear, if not new, to merit a brief review of them here. Christians along with Jews would affirm the two-edged nature of God's Word in the poles of judgment and grace. The wilderness experience stands alongside the return to the Promised Land in the same way that Good Friday stands alongside Easter. Irrespective of particular Christian traditions, it is most often the grace or "gospel" (Good News) that gets shortchanged. An ongoing proclamation of law is the frequent result. The importance of a twofold understanding is stressed by Gerhard Ebeling:

> This means that making the distinction in practice between the law and the gospel is not fortuitous and incidental to the process of preaching, but is what really is meant to take place within it. But if the process of preaching is what it claims to be, that is, the process of salvation, then as the distinction is made between the law and the gospel, so the event of salvation takes place. And a confusion between the two is not a misfortune of little significance, a regrettable weakness, but is evil in the strict sense, the total opposite of salvation.[4]

The reasons for the confusion that happens in so many pulpits go beyond lack of understanding. Some have to do with our inclination as preachers to dispense God's judgment as the essence of Christian preaching ("You tell them, preacher!"). Some of the confusion may also have to do with the difficulty in finding good news in many of the texts from which we preach. And some may simply point to the influence of the world's view on our own: the world does not speak or see with authentic hope.

The starting place for understanding law and gospel is the ancient Jewish understanding of law. The Hebrew word "Torah" came to be universally understood as "law," although the synonyms for it such as "word," "commandment," "testimony," or "teaching" remove it from the more limited understanding we have derived from the Latin *lex*. For the Jews, law was no hair shirt or burden, for law was a gift and privilege since through it people discovered their responsibility to God. Praising God was the purpose of life and the law made this a possibility. We often misunderstand the Jewish idea of law if we think of it as a heavy backpack to be carried and count with ever-widening eyes the number of weighty instructions it contains. Walter Brueggemann contrasts our misunderstanding with the freedom the law actually represents for Jewish people.

> Torah that marks the new community is not a practice of law to clobber people, not a censure to expel and scold people, not a picky legalism. It is rather a release from small moralisms to see things through the eyes of God's passion and anguish. The Torah is a reminder that God's will focuses on large human concerns and that we also may focus on weighty matters of justice, mercy and righteousness.[5]

Torah was a route to community freedom in relationship to God.

It was Jesus who upbraided the contemporary teachers for giving a tenth of even their spices like mint, dill, and cumin, but neglecting to give due emphasis to the really "important matters of the law—justice, mercy and faithfulness" (Matt. 23:23). Here we see the tension between the laws in themselves and the goal of the laws. It is similar to the tension Christians experience between giving obedience to the law and practicing their Christian freedom in faith and forgiveness. This tension was felt by Paul, who argued that obedience was insufficient for salvation; by Augustine, whose "love God and do as you wish," has often been quoted as a justification for the immoral living he opposed; and in varying degrees by others in the course of the centuries.

We need not wade too far into the thicket of Roman Catholic and Protestant differences on law and gospel. Protestants paid more attention to these terms (although not necessarily to what they represent) in part because some of Luther's claims like *sola scriptura* (scripture is to be interpreted by written scripture alone, not by unwritten tradition), *sola fide* (saved by faith alone), and *sola gratia* (saved by God's grace alone) were aimed at separating divine law from canon law and at a clarification of the role of grace. For Luther there were two uses of law: (a) law in its civil or political use, to deter people from acts of wickedness by threat of punishment, and (b) law in its theological use, to make people conscious of their responsibilities and thus repentant of their sins. To these another reformer, John Calvin, added a third use, an excitement to obedience, which comes close to some of the Jewish notions of Torah.

Catholic understanding has varied, but takes exception to the exclusivity of the *sola* claim. Canon law is not identified as divine law but nonetheless has a stature above secular polity and can provide a route to salvation. This represents some of the positive view of law inherent in Torah. It has also led to the use of the terms "church" and "grace," often in preference to "gospel," and the use of "judgment" instead of "law." Grace resides in the created order, thus good works are possible from human initiative.

As Dominic Grasso, S. J., has put it, "Even if fallen from the dignity with which God surrounded [human nature] in creation, even if wounded in its natural gifts and weakened, it retains its relationship with God, its ultimate goal, and its ability to work some good."[6] But as Grasso also demonstrates, "law and gospel" are not foreign to Catholics. He talks about the relation of "laws of reality," which he also calls "system," to the Good News "message": "While the system is thus static and conservative because it limits itself to seeing reality as it is, the message is dynamic and revolutionary because it attempts to upset an existing situation in order to create another. The system creates resignation; the message, hope. It is a Gospel, the Good Tidings, the Good News that the reality of things can become better."[7]

And as Edward Schillebeeckx points out, the use of the term "gospel" in Roman theology is on the increase: "Whereas in the past appeal would have been made primarily to 'the church' . . . it is now customary to invoke 'the gospel.' "[8]

The differences, although complex and deep-rooted, need not muddy the biblical distinctions that both traditions affirm between law and gospel or judgment and grace. One of the most important of these for preaching is that *there are two kinds of law: the one we all know, and the other which many of us have not named*. The kind of law we know is what may be called the law as

chastiser, to use Paul's metaphor of law as severe
tutor ("paidagogos") in Galatians 3:24, or "fire
and brimstone" law, or "hierarchical" law. *This
familiar kind of law is what Herman G. Stuempfle
calls, "law as Hammer of Judgment,"*[9] taking a
metaphor from Luther, law which smashes our
pretensions and brings us to our knees in prayer.
We might equally call it the "law as hammer of
righteousness," since it represents a call to
morality that is in itself an impossible task. This
"kind" of law speaks to the conscience and warns
of punishment that might be ours.

Obviously this is a severe notion of law to
preach. *A special kind of gospel is needed in relation
to this kind of law. It is the gospel of forgiveness and
love.* But for some people this harsh notion of law
is the entire sum of their early Christian experience, and the forgiveness spoken about was never
experienced. We might ask, of course, "If law has
been heard apart from grace, has God's law been
heard or it is merely some shadow of God's
Word?" The real point, however, is that these
people understood it to be God speaking to them.
It is hard for these people to imagine that
preaching law could be anything but bitter. But if
care is taken to ensure that a balanced structure is
present that has the possibility of bearing grace,
the sweet cream of love and forgiveness may be
lavishly poured out. God's Word is always
judgment and grace, law and gospel.

*The other kind of law that has gone unnoticed by
many of us is equally biblical but less commonly
named as law. We might call this the law of the Fall;
or the law of the world; or the law of human systems.*
Stuempfle calls this other kind of law, "law as

mirror of existence" because it mirrors life as we know it, fallen and broken as it is. In other words, simply to describe the pain we see in the faces of the hungry, to talk about the innocent being crucified, or to show how good people unknowingly do evil—this is to preach the law of the world. It mirrors life. It is the judgment upon us that we already experience as a consequence of our sin. Said another way, the conditions in which we find ourselves mark our fallenness and cause us to seek remedy. This is the law by which we see the consequences of relying upon our own resources, a law whose effective power is our captivity. *It is never merely a description of the world around us, however. It is always a description in anticipation of the countering Word of God.*

This kind of law that mirrors existence may be our normal, but not exclusive, goal in providing a structure that enables law, simply because in today's world the other law, law as hammer of judgment, is frequently regarded with suspicion, even by many faithful Christians. People today are annoyed with constant loud knocking at the door of a guilty conscience that refuses to answer. (It is even possible that "guilt-tripping" may prompt guilt to take a trip!) We cannot keep hitting our people with the law as a hammer. If we want to reach people with the gospel, we must understand them: "There are many—and they may form a majority in the contemporary world—for whom guilt is not the primary category by which they define their situation. They resonate more immediately to such terms as meaninglessness, anxiety, despair, or alienation."[10]

The gospel as forgiveness does not really meet

these cries. *The gospel that links with this kind of law may be conceived or structured as that which overturns the world.* For the wandering one there is now a home; for the anxious one there is now a soothing voice to calm the night; for the desperate one there is more hope than the soul can contain; and for the one who has been hurt too many times there are the open arms of friends gathered around a table.

Preachers who are exploring law and gospel for the first time might be cautioned against three common errors my students sometimes make. We may place three caution signs around the study desk or the pulpit for the preacher to see.

The first says, *"We do not want to become legalistic concerning the gospel, turning it into a new set of laws that must be followed."* The gospel is an invitation to fullness of life through faith in Jesus Christ. We respond to the difficult times not with the certainty of knowledge for which we, like the disciples, often long. "Where will we find you?" we cry, "Tell us the way." We want definite answers and an absence of ambiguity. But Jesus refuses to provide all of the specific answers. He refuses those things that would turn following him into a code of behavior, that in themselves would form a kind of law alone, cut off from gospel, and that would dispense with the necessity of pursuing him as the Living Savior. Jesus responds "I am the Way." It is an invitation to faith. When we speak of grace or gospel, we will not be prescribing a solution that *we* discern through *our* wisdom but rather will be inviting people into the mystery of death overcome in the reconciling action of Christ.

The second sign says that *"God is a present reality in the realms of both law and gospel."* The law that mirrors our lives and the gospel that overturns the world do not divide reality into a world where God is not and a world where God is. Jesus Christ is found in our broken world as much as in the vision we receive from the gospel of how this world is to be—and reigns over them both.

The third caution, which we have already discussed at some length, reads, *"Law and gospel at times fuse together."* Absolute distinction is not for us to have. Many grasp for a certainty in identifying the Old Testament as law and the New Testament as gospel, when in fact law and gospel are contained in each of the Testaments. The Word is two-edged and we cannot always be sure which edge is which. While we may seem to be able in our experience to separate law and gospel, and while we will be setting in place structures to enable each, they are in fact so interrelated as to be theologically co-present. Luther said there was no one "living on earth who knows how to distinguish between the Law and the Gospel. We may think we understand it when we're listening to a sermon, but we're far from it. Only the Holy Spirit knows this."[11] Similarly we may think we understand the difference when we are preparing to preach, but each is sounded in the chord of the other. There is what Richard Lischer has called a "fluidity of law and gospel." "Thus the death of Jesus reveals God's wrath *and* love; the call to discipleship both stings and encourages the Christian."[12]

Our goal, therefore, is to preach in such a way that this fluidity is enhanced. We have a task to do that we cannot simply leave to the Holy Spirit. We will develop structures to facilitate the reception of both law and gospel. We do so in what Kierkegaard called "fear and trembling," and we wait on the Lord. The process of establishing structures to enhance law and gospel can be assisted if we remember that, since each is present in the other, the most we can be striving for is not an exclusive identification but what seems to be a predominant and potential one.

Practical Helps

Our role is not to create law and gospel, for God's Word already exists as both. That is its nature. When Moses found only condemnation for Israel in God's Word, he rebuked God and God recanted. God's Word is always bifocal: it never exists alone as law or alone as gospel. To use another image, it is a loaf of bread that we are to break open: the separation of potential law and gospel or judgment and grace, although they are one, is made in order that we may show their reconciliation, that our lives may witness to their wholeness. It was in the breaking of the bread that Jesus was known by the disciples.

Most discussions of our topic hesitate to give practical guidance as to how we might separate or distinguish the two when dealing with a particular biblical text. Let us turn to some practical aids to help us distinguish the law-gospel poles in our preaching; later we will have space to make some particular suggestions through examining one biblical text in detail.

1. We can be clear that *at the simplest level, law,*

although a gift, places the burden on us, requiring us to do something. Morris Niedenthal is getting at this when he says, "It presupposes strength but does nothing to create it."[13] In Deuteronomy 30:11 ff., God sets before Israel the choice between blessing and curse. It is a choice which is "not too difficult for you or beyond your reach." The burden, however bearable, still rests with the people. One of the recurrent themes of the Bible is that we fail to bear even that which is bearable. *Gospel, on the other hand, at its simplest level places the burden on God, and God has already accepted that burden in Jesus Christ.* Gospel, "does not presuppose strength but seeks to create it by ministering to need and weakness."[14] It removes for us all the barriers that previously stood in our way of responding to God's Word and discloses to us a new future. A common error is to think that judgment in preaching is good news, since it is only by judgment that we can find the route to salvation. Judgment has a grace dimension, but nonetheless remains judgment. What feels like a burden resting upon us generally is a burden. Similarly, what doesn't strike us as good news generally may not be good news.

2. To be God's Word preaching needs a balance between law and gospel. A sermon or homily that avoids law gives what Bonhoeffer called "cheap grace"—which is no grace at all. It disregards the price that Christ paid for our salvation. Perhaps we would do better to speak of preaching that omits the potential law as a "pep-talk" or "hints toward optimism" and preaching that skips the potential gospel as a "guilt-trip" or a "secular essay on despair."

Most preaching that we hear spends most of the time on law and perhaps toward the end, in the last minute or two, moves to what might be the Good News. The Good News is doled out as though there is a shortage of God's love. It is rather tragic if our sermons and homilies only turn to Good News in the final minute, for it is then the law, not the Good News, which worshipers carry away with them. In such preaching there may be little imagination that will kindle faith. The Good News may be culled from the biblical text and brought to the fore from a point midway in the preaching if it is to be heard and appropriated by the congregation. Good news is not good news until it has the same relevance, the same degree of concreteness, the same compelling identification, the same immediacy as the law is given. *A fifty-fifty balance between law and gospel (which in practical reality may vary from week to week between sixty-forty or forty-sixty) may seem radical, given what we have been used to, but it is a worthy ideal.* It establishes the poles clearly, with plenty of potential energy and spark.

3. There is a natural movement in the Christian faith from law *to* gospel, from judgment *to* grace, from Exodus *to* Promised Land, and from Good Friday *to* Easter. The movement is not reversed, nor is it back and forth, the to and fro wearing each other out like two parts of an old hinge. Rather, it is a progression that marks God's continuing restorative promise to the world. The same natural flow might be our normal goal in structuring preaching. First comes the law, then comes the gospel. We want each to be heard in strength, each to be heard as dominant, not each drowned out by the other, or one heard at the expense of the other. Structuring the preaching as a movement from law to gospel of course need not guarantee that the Spirit will use it this way. It is the Bible, however, that prescribes the movement for us. To assist, we may recognize that conditional statements about the gospel are law, and they may belong in the law section.

When we arrive at the gospel section, our statements can be without condition. The conditions of salvation are already established and developed: judgment may be mentioned briefly in passing, but should not be explored in any detail, for that should have been done already. Consider discarding phrases like, "I believe" or "I think," since these are automatically conditional. Consider taking statements like, "If we repent," or "If we do this," out of the gospel section and simply returning them to the law section. When the gospel is only stated conditionally it is never fully released. How strange it would be to serve someone the communion bread and then take it back and say, "Are you sure you are ready for this?" There is no need. Neither is there a need in the sermon or homily to be ungenerous in the grace Christ is offering.

4. Every text contains law and gospel, judgment and grace. This radical idea is not as strange as it may at first appear. Some of us were traded a poor understanding of the bifocal Word when we were told in college or seminary that a text might have only law and that therefore the preaching would have only law. *When we find only law or judgment in a text, it is not that good news is not present, it is that we are seeing less with the eyes of*

faith than with the eyes of the world. The world
trains us to see without authentic hope, and
without a linking of judgment and hope. But as
Christians we read every biblical text through the
cross and resurrection. Finding potential law
may often be easy. But to find potential gospel in
every text often requires training—yet it is there
as surely as there is light in every day. This
understanding can open many new doors for us.
We need never despair with the heavy weight of a
particular Bible text if we can learn the truth of
this. It is a skilled thing to teach or preach Good
News.

5. Statements of conventional wisdom and also
questions in general may be classified as forms of
law although they are often confused with gospel.
The one is cliché and the other hammers away, but
both put the burden on us. Slogans of conventional
wisdom have received their authenticity from the
world, not from the Scriptures. Such slogans
include: "Only the good die young"; "Might makes
right"; "If you work hard you will succeed";
"Success is getting to the top"; "The only good Red
is a dead Red"; and any number of similar lines
that have been used to justify events or to explain
what happened. The words of these sayings are
rooted in the dead word of the world.

If a sermon or homily on the Good Samaritan
only asks the question, Who is our neighbor? the
gospel has not been reached. Questions put the
burdens on us with the largest burdens being
picked up by the most sensitive souls. The gospel
does not and cannot provide us with absolute
answers, for absolutes are a kind of law, but it
does invite us into the possibility of a decision in

faith that is filled with hope and offers the confidence and joy of acting in faith. Ask questions in the law section but be careful asking them from the gospel section. Your proclamation will be assisted and the congregation enabled with the light burden of God's Word.

6. Whether we realize it or not, some gestures and words are law, inescapably law. A wagging finger, a pointed finger, a raised fist, anger or bellowing or a monotone voice are law gestures. Commands like "must," "should," "have to," "realize," and numerous other imperative words and phrases are law. They may have their place in the first half, but not in the last half. Part of the beauty of the gospel is that it is invitational, not demanding. It is light, in the manner of the Jesus' parables, not burdensome. It is direct, in the manner of a child's gentle hand leading us to explore. Simply going through the gospel section of our sermons or homilies and changing a few words can alter the entire tone: "must" changes to "may"; "should" changes to "can" or "are now able"; "have to" changes to "there is no longer any barrier preventing us"; "realize" changes to "we now see" or "it is clear to us." These words are invitational and affirming, not reproving. They lift us up instead of dragging us down.

7. Good news belongs in the present. When the good news lies only in the future, law is the message. The good news for too many people lies only in the future. We may say, "We have already repented" (pointing to our baptism or to communion) instead of, "We must repent"; "We have already changed, even in this moment" instead of, "You must change"; "There is now nothing

separating us from God's love," instead of "God
will love us when we—." Genuine proclamation
of the gospel, if it is to sound like good news,
requires the present tense, the immediacy of right
now. Good news becomes better news if it is
available in this second, in the already accom-
plished present. Good news should sound like
good news.

Law and gospel are linked. Together they are
the spark of God's Word. Split apart from each
other, they cannot exist except as shadows, faint
outlines of a form, as our lives are like shadows
when we feel separated from God's Word. But
when law and gospel are bound together, we find
ourselves unbound and holding to God's Word for
that freedom that unites us with all people, as we
can only be united by God. But let us now see how
we use these homiletical tools with specific texts.

Taking the First Steps

In the previous chapter we began working on
concerns of the text (defined as ideas with which
the text is legitimately concerned, short sentences
arising from the story and exegesis of the text,
specific to the details of the text) and concerns of
the sermon/homily (defined as the concerns of the
text transposed from biblical time to now
through generalizing the textual details). We
begin using these tools first by separating
concerns of the text into law and gospel. Then we
can consider in greater depth the subject of
transposing.

To demonstrate, let us consider the wedding at
Cana in John 2:1-11. Let us assume that we have

experienced the story of the text and that what interests us about the story is that, "Mary expected Jesus to do a miracle." That becomes our first guess about the meaning. In our exegesis we might turn to two of the best commentaries on John, the ones by Bultmann and by Raymond Brown. Among the ideas noted in our thumbnail exegesis could be the following, which we may list as concerns of the text:

Mary, Jesus, and the disciples were at the wedding.

The wedding was by invitation.

It was a celebration.

Either the preparations were inadequate, *or* more guests showed up than expected, *or* the partying went on longer than anticipated. (Each of these being a possibility justified by the shortage of wine.)

The wine ran out.

Mary noticed the absence of wine. (Our first guess was proven an inauthentic interpretation as verse 5 might imply no more than her expectation that Jesus would run out to get some wine.)

Mary is taking care of the celebration.

Jesus appears indifferent. (This avoids saying he was annoyed at his mother's comment which would be psychologizing the text.)

Jesus hears his mother's remark in connection to his ministry.

Jesus indicates the absence of wine has little to do with him.

(Is he implying that creation of new wine, prior to his "hour," is for God alone?)

Jesus creates the best wine.
Jesus is on the side of celebration.
The miracle indicates Christ's risen glory. (See
        the reference to "on the third day" and the
        communion parallels.)
Now is the time of Christ's glory ("hour").

From the initial reading of the biblical text we
can be alert to possible law and gospel concerns.
These may scarcely seem able to bear the
theological freight we might try to attach to them.
But it is rather like looking at a child and
imagining what she will look like when older; we
look at these ideas and dream what meaning they
might carry in the preaching itself. They are
dislodged from the text for the benefit of
imagination. They may have only a slight whiff of
law or gospel about them but now is the time for
dreaming, not for experimenting and testing.

Bearing in mind the "fluidity of law and
gospel," we might be open to the possibility that
some concerns might fit either category, depend-
ing in part on how we chose to develop them for
preaching. But also bearing in mind that we are
trained by the world to see a law cut off from
gospel, not law and gospel, we need not be
surprised if we do not immediately find good
news in a text. It is important to acknowledge this
if it occurs. Sometimes a particular law concern is
rubbing us so abrasively that gospel seems
impossible. We will come later to ways of getting
out of such difficulties.

Some of the above list of concerns of the text for
the wedding at Cana might be divided in the
following way:

LAW CONCERNS OF THE TEXT	GOSPEL CONCERNS OF THE TEXT
Attendance was by invitation.	Jesus was at the wedding.
More guests came than were expected (or gospel?).	More guests came than were expected (or law?).
Preparation was inadequate.	Water into wine is God's work.
The guests ran out of wine.	Jesus is on the side of celebration.
The absence was noticed.	With Jesus present the celebration does not end.
The celebration was in danger of ending.	Jesus reveals himself.
Jesus appears indifferent.	The risen Christ is in glory.
It was not Jesus' "hour."	Now is the time of Jesus' glory.
Mary was taking care of the party.	

Each biblical text is like a cut diamond with many sides. Listing the concern of the text allows us to see many facets of each. We could focus on this text from the viewpoint of Mary, or the guests, or the absence of wine, or Jesus, or even the empty stone jars. In preaching we might intentionally shift the congregational identification from one person or perspective to another, not in a confusing way, but each in measured succession. It is a good thing to remember that whenever we identify our people as Christ, this forms a powerful good news idea; it is wonderful to think that through our actions in the world we, as God's people, can each turn water into wine.

Transposing

Now let us go back again to the subject of transposing. We began this at the end of the last chapter where we dealt with Zacchaeus, but now we will do so from the perspective of law and gospel. Once more we will feel the energy of the text working in us and for us, and we will sense the sermon or homily starting to write itself. Soon we will be ready to establish the overall law-gospel polarity for preaching.

The following transpositions of concerns of the text into concerns of the sermon/homily include some of my own reflections as my imagination works for me. We want to be open to the Spirit speaking to us and inspiring us through the sparking. Here there will be examples given of transposing a second or third time to produce greater tension, a wider gap, a bigger spark. Theoretically we may rephrase and transpose a concern of the text as many times as we want, as long as we do not lose the connection to the original text. A secondary or alternate transposition does not mean the first one was unworthy, but is rather shown here to suggest the range of possibilities that can be opened up for imagination and faith.

1. Transposing Law

Abbreviations: **T** = concern of the text; **S** = concern of the sermon/homily

T: The preparations were inadequate.

S: Our preparations are often inadequate (transposition 1). (What experiences of this come to mind? We know of tragedies no amount of preparation could have avoided.)

Or **S2:** The preparations of those who suffer are always inadequate (transposition 2). (The plight of our brothers and sisters and some Christian social analysis will be appropriate to the law section.)

* * *

T: The wine ran out.

S: Our wine runs out (transposition 1). (Little tension is with text.)

Or **S2:** Our good times end (transposition 2). (Here I have used "wine" as an image for our good times; this is consistent with the text. Good times ending is the way of the world.)

Or **S3:** Good times have ended for the unemployed (transposition 3). (Either S2 or S3 would be strong.)

* * *

T: The absence of wine was noticed.

S: Our absence is rarely noticed (transposition 1).

Or **S2:** The absence of the poor is rarely noticed (transposition 2). (What this might mean is not immediately obvious to me, but somewhere in here the truth may be nibbling. I might decide to go after it in the preaching to see what it looks like.)

* * *

T: The guests missed the wine (similar to the above).

S: We miss what we do not have.

* * *

T: Jesus appears indifferent to his mother's comment.

S: Jesus appears indifferent to our prayers (transposition 1). (This will be a powerful concern to develop in the law section, particularly if juxtaposed with a gospel concern of this text, "Jesus was not indifferent to the need.")

Or S2: We are indifferent to Jesus' will (transposition 2). (A half-truth. The conditions we place on this in the preaching can make it a whole truth. There are many instances of this apparent indifference.)

2. Transposing Gospel

T: Jesus was at the wedding.

S: Jesus is present in our celebrations. (Again a half-truth. While Christ is present in all our celebrations of authentic life, would we celebrate that which should not be celebrated? Perhaps we would, but Christ may be weeping—but this is the sermon or homily starting to write itself.)

* * *

T: Mary was taking care of the party.

S: God is nurturing the world. (Is this true? What evidence in addition to the scriptural attestation do we have or do we know this only in faith? If we know something in faith, do we not see things in faith?)

* * *

T: Water into wine is God's work.

S: Wherever miracles happen, God is present.

T: Jesus turns water into wine.

S: Jesus turns our sorrows into joy (transposition 1). (Slightly too facile, in danger of skimming over the depth of suffering in the world. The goal of the faith is not to be happy, *per se*, but to be a faithful witness to God's love, one fruit of which might well be joy.)

Or S2: Jesus turns the pain of the world into the cup of his suffering (transposition 2). (This adopts the eucharistic hint in the text in substituting "cup of suffering" for "wine." It gets closer to an idea we would affirm but it may still need some work: God is with us in our suffering. This could lead to a useful discussion of God's saving action.)

* * *

T: With Jesus present the celebration does not end.

S: In Christ there is unending hope for the world. (The concern of the text simply indicates that the wedding celebration was able to continue. In the concern of the sermon/homily we are elevating the "does not end" hint to eschatological proportion.)

* * *

T: Jesus reveals himself to the disciples.

S: Jesus reveals himself to us (or to the world, to those in need, to the suffering, to the oppressed).

* * *

T: The risen Christ is in glory.

S: We already participate in Christ's glory.
            (What might this mean? What might be
            hopeful in this for the person suffering
            cancer?)

Preparing to preach is exciting. The list of
juxtapositions we have just been noting is only a
beginning. Each one of us could add more, and
each of our parishioners could lead us to still
further ones. Preaching a biblical text is like going
to a grocery store: we could always find something else we could use. The shifting of one word,
like moving the wrong apple in the display, can
change the whole arrangement. One different
word can make a new concern of the text or
concern of the sermon/homily. We may be
beginning to sense how vast is the arena of
authentic interpretation. It would be difficult to
exhaust the meaning of a text. Even if we were
using the lectionary and using many of the same
texts every three years, the end products could be
quite different. The list we have here already
contains more text-situation units than we could
develop fully in any one sermon or homily—there
would not be time. We are simply spreading
before us a wide selection from which we will
choose what we want.

As with most things that are new, it is in the
doing that we begin to understand. Try transposing law and gospel with a text of your own. You
might keep in mind that some of the concerns you
record could be slightly altered to enhance either
the potential law or gospel. For example, if a law
concern of the sermon/homily says, "We must not
judge," we may choose to go with this idea (law as

hammer of judgment) or we may find we have more to say with a transposition such as, "We feel judged by the world" (law as mirror of existence). To take another example, if for a concern of the sermon/homily we have, "God invites us to live out the Commandments," we have a concern that might seem to be good news. But it would be stronger if it was not simply an invitation; an invitation can still be refused. It would be better to say instead, "God enables us to live out the Commandments." The burden is more firmly placed on God. Similarly, "Jesus calls us to new life," would be better phrased, "Jesus gives us new life."

Law, Gospel, and Homiletical Structure

We said earlier that all powerful biblical preachers develop text-situation poles. While for most of us the process is not automatic, we may nonetheless come up with more imaginative and powerful linkings than we would if we scooted past on intuition's skateboard. Similarly, many great biblical preachers also have the spark in their preaching that already exists in the faith, in the tension between cross and resurrection. That there should be this dialogue between cross and resurrection is one of the great grammatical rules of preaching, however infrequently it may be observed in practice. God's Word itself is a reconciliation of the opposites of law and gospel. When the structures for law and gospel in preaching are in relationship to each other, yet sufficiently far apart to allow each to be experienced on its own, we provide the opportunity for hearers to experience the hope and promise of the faith. But again, because homiletics may have been excessively intuitive in the past without always paying sufficient attention to language and technical skill, most preachers lack this spark that could overarch the sermon or homily.

One way of visualizing the communication process is the reduction, representation, expansion cycle we talked about earlier. Because this is a repeating pattern of moving in, crystallizing meaning, and moving out—a pattern that repeats at every level of the communication process—it can be understood as a circle. It may be similar to Friederich Schleiermacher's "hermeneutical circle": we understand a biblical text by moving in and out of it over and over until we have a sense of the whole. The movement is a repeating circle. We have all experienced this circle when translating a written text or in reading a difficult passage; we read it over and over again until it begins to make sense.

Similarly, the structure of the sermon or homily may be conceived as a circle. When picturing how to create the spark of law and

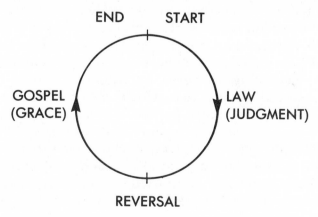

gospel or judgment and grace for preaching, this may be the most helpful image. We begin at the top and move down through the law or judgment. By the time we reach the lowest point we have also reached the depth of our awareness of our sin. The lowest point is the reversal point. From here on our direction is reversed as we develop the gospel or grace that overturns the world. The possibility of creating a spark is enhanced by the simple juxtaposition of these two movements.

The reversal point is the containing wall that holds back the predominance of law from gospel. I will be developing a variety of forms for sermons or homilies in later chapters. Newer approaches to preaching tend to understand preaching structure as modular, however, not static. This basic circle is an idea we will want to retain and develop further.

It is possible that the law-gospel spark may be achieved in preaching by more frequent law-gospel juxtapositions instead of the simple format I am suggesting here as a normative guide. On the odd occasion an alternative might be tried. Most often when I have seen this tried, however, the flow of the preaching is repeatedly broken; neither law nor gospel is treated with clarity; and the gospel each time becomes so closely linked to a specific law situation that it is in danger of degenerating to become mere problem-solving.

Each of us has experienced the law-gospel spark in our lives. There are frequent times when we are pressured by too many issues, some so worthy of attention they cannot be let go and others so unworthy we hang on to them in the fear they say the truth about us. The greater the pressure, the more strained are all things, and the more brittle and fragile we become. It is at these times that we know what it means to be living under the law. When the spark of law and gospel or judgment and grace is experienced in a substantial way, there is hope where there was despair, or reconciliation where there was alienation, or forgiveness where there was guilt and sorrow.

Our congregations have need of this spark. When they gather on Sunday with the sharp lines of the week on their faces and hands, they want to know they have been seen and heard. They want to know that somehow they have been recognized, acknowledged to be present, and addressed with special words just for them. The law-gospel structure should assist this. During the law section of the preaching, which gathers up the shards of life that have fallen around the community and the world, the congregation shows a dawning recognition that what is being said, is not about two thousand years ago, but is about right now, about them in the focus of God's love. The more they recognize the broken pieces as pieces from their own lives, the more open they are to being touched. The more they recognize their own hunger, the more they long for the food that is prepared for them. Thus in terms of our limited control, when the heart of the biblical text's good news is proclaimed, it leaps forward to people eager for it. They are saying to themselves, "Could it possibly be true? Might hope still be for me? Is there yet life ahead?" When such unimagined grace is experienced, people rush toward it. Such is the nature of God's Word moving in the congregation.

Each sermon or homily can contain a variety of law and gospel concerns. When this is the case the structural tension between law and gospel is not reconciled immediately (as would be the case if a law concern were immediately counterbalanced with a gospel concern). Rather the tension is allowed to mount until the second half, when the sparking will take place. Which particular text-situation units will be chosen will matter less than that structures enabling law and gospel to be heard are clearly developed. The overarching spark may happen irrespective of the particular units finally selected (in other words, direct or immediate counterpoints do not always have to be designed). The structural process is simple, not complex. How rigid we will be in following it, in trying to keep law and gospel as separate as we are able, will be up to the individual preacher. But if this guideline is kept in mind as a goal worth aiming for, it can have a dramatic effect in improving our preaching.

What is distinctive about this approach to homiletical movement is, first, its simplicity. There are a variety of ways in which other writers have conceived of a similar kind of law-gospel movement. Some of these are helpful, although they can obscure the simplicity of the basic movement involved. A few are worth citing. Milton Crum, for instance, agrees that the structure should, "move from fallen humanity to redeemed humanity, from sin to faith, from darkness to light, from what Paul calls living 'according to the flesh' to living 'according to the spirit,' from condemnation to justification, from alienation to sanctification."[15] His approach becomes more complicated, however, when, to accomplish this, he suggests employing "Dynamic Factors" in a threefold movement: situation (which develops a symptomatic behavior needing change), complication (which gets at the root cause and resulting consequences), and a resolution (the content of the gospel gives a new way of perceiving and believing).[16]

Eugene L. Lowry has a similar movement, which has five rather than three stages: upsetting the equilibrium, analyzing the discrepancy, disclosing the key to resolution, experiencing the gospel, and anticipating the consequences.[17] Robert P. Waznak, who like Lowry is also interested in narrative form, borrows from a number of people in suggesting that the homily is a combination of three stories (the stories of the listener, of the preacher, and of God) that starts in "lost hope" (the story of the listener or the preacher), moves to interpretation of the text, and ends in the "new hope" of our stories seen in the light of God's story.[18]

And Deane A. Kemper uses a three-stage progression developed by Henry Babcock Adams, from question (introduction) to assertion (body) to invitation (conclusion).[19] Helpful though each of these approaches may be, I am not yet personally convinced, in relation to the simple law-gospel movement being developed here, that they are necessary.

What may also be distinctive about this approach in addition to its simplicity, is that it is both biblical and theological. It is biblical in that it is firmly planted in the soil of the biblical text. It is theological in that the method derives from the categories of law and gospel. Sometimes the categories advocated for homiletical method seem more related to psychology or marketing than they do to the faith. Or often, when categories like law and gospel are used to describe homiletical method, the law may be incorrectly suggested to be "our word" (which is then countered by "God's Word"), or the gospel is treated as though it is a mere answer to our problems, rather than a living and independent redemptive Word.

The Reversal Point and the Central Idea

The movement of a sermon or homily is appropriately understood if it is thought of as dance. I am thinking here of the carefully choreographed, well-rehearsed, artful dance that flows and tumbles like a mountain stream. Of necessity we have been developing technical language to deal with what could partly be understood as a form of art in honor of the Creator. Whether we are talking about art theory or homiletical theory for imagination, theory in and of itself is technical. And as in any art, theory is an attempt to get at the basics by suggesting basic rules—these can be violated, but to maximize creativity, to ensure that creative energies are focused in the right areas, these basics can stand as general norms. But we do not want to forget that it is the dance of God's Word that we are after. Our efforts should seem spontaneous, effortless, and free-flowing, yet at the same time profound and moving.

A key element in this process is the choreographing of the turning point or the reversal. When we move into the gospel section, we structure the reversal as an overturning of the world, a reversal of our expectations, and an action of God's inbreaking realm.[20] To set up this movement it is necessary to identify the central idea of the sermon or homily.

John Killinger and James W. Cox, whose recent books of similar title each give a fresh review of preaching, speak in familiar ways about the importance of the central idea. Killinger suggests that the central idea arises most often out of the preacher's notebooks that should be carried constantly, written in as often as an idea for preaching occurs, and reviewed and harvested frequently.[21]

James Cox has further useful suggestions. The characteristics of a central idea he outlines as follows: it will be relevant ("stated in timeless language"); complete ("it should contain the essence of the entire sermon, both subject and predicate") simple "avoid heavy theological or philosophical language"); lean ("omitting unnecessary adjectives and adverbs as well as unnecessary qualifying phrases and clauses"); striking ("able to be fixed in the hearer's memory . . . [and] brief; the longer the sentence, the fuzzier the meaning and the more difficult the remembering"); and literal ("figurative language sometimes obscures the thought or commits the preacher to pursue a dominant image"). Concerning this latter point, Cox, like so many, unfortunately does not honor the way in which figurative language, carefully used, can clarify thought and open new understandings, or the way in which a dominant image can be used powerfully to unify a sermon or homily. Examples of what he thinks are good central ideas include: "Good intentions are no excuse for bad actions," "Faithfulness in present duty qualifies for higher functions," and "Obligation to God is a privilege."[22]

What is useful in this approach is the insistence that the central message be absolutely clear, simple, and short (we have been saying something similar in relation to the various concerns of the text) and that the beginning of writing a sermon or homily is to write out this statement. What is wrong is equally apparent.

First, many of the central ideas we find in contemporary preaching have no relation to the biblical text. Sometimes they are ideas taken to a particular biblical text that is then bent to reinforce them. Sometimes they are simply the favorite themes of the preacher which, even when developed in the preaching, end up as moral, social, or theological platitudes.

Second, there is no suggestion that the central idea should be an idea of good news, which may be why so much preaching ends up as predominantly law or judgment. Cox's ideas, above, lack inherent good news.

Third, the source of the central idea remains largely mystical. As Killinger says, "The preacher's mind will be hovering over the text . . . suddenly a single shaft of light will penetrate the murkiness, and that light will become the center of the world—or, in this case, the sermon."[23] We may all recognize what Killinger is talking about, but description of an experience the preacher is supposed to have does not help the preacher who is unable to have it. We need practical guidelines, technical guidelines, to ensure that imagination does not remain in the category of the mystical. Partly because I am here assuming that preaching will be biblical preaching, and partly because we are paying attention to how language functions, more precise direction is possible.

In keeping with the theory I have been developing, I will suggest that *the central idea actually consists of two ideas, one arising from the biblical text. We will call this the major concern of the text. Its transposed good news concern of the sermon/homily we will call the major concern of the sermon/homily.*

To determine your central idea, choose from your list of gospel concerns one that interests you, prods you and shows you a glimpse of something you never dreamed of before. It may even be one that rubs you the wrong way or one you anticipate members of your congregation will react against. Whatever other features this will have, it needs to be fresh and intriguing for you: if it does not first interest you, it will interest no one else. There is not just one idea around which any text is focused. There are many ideas and each can open the biblical text in an appropriate manner; we have already determined that the list of gospel concerns of the text in front of us are true to the text. Having chosen which gospel concern this is, we simply elevate it in its two parts (the concern of the text and the concern of the sermon/homily), to major status in our minds. It is major because we choose to make it so simply by giving it the central focus in our preaching. Any text can address any situation.

It is wonderful to trust the text to give birth to the idea and then to trust ourselves to be able to use the text's prodding to speak to whatever situation needs to be addressed.

The banana peel for most preaching, the slippery place where most slip, is in the choice and timing of the central idea. Many fine preachers start to write without knowing what their central idea will be. But sometimes even fine preachers get caught never having found their central idea. What we are suggesting here can make for more efficient use of preparation time and greater focus from the outset. In terms of the preaching week we are only on Tuesday, still early, yet with our focus already determined. Other fine preachers at times are content to allow their central idea simply to be a crucial question. By insisting here that the idea be a complete, good news thought we attempt to avoid the inevitable predominance of law that results from such question-posing. If the major concern of the text is not a complete sentence or thought (i.e., "the way Jesus loves" instead of saying what that way is, such as, "Jesus invites you to celebrate"), or if the idea is not precise (i.e., "how Jesus acts at the wedding"), or if the idea is law not gospel, a fall is predictable.

The major concern of the text is always a gospel concern. It takes skill to give equal structural emphasis to law and gospel since a kind of law, split from gospel, is our normal way of seeing things. But if we start from a law perspective with the central idea, our balance is already lost and the sermon or homily we had hoped would do great things will simply crash, spilling the meal and breaking the plates.

One other qualification is helpful in choosing a major concern of the text from the various gospel concerns: choose one that focuses on an action of Jesus or an action of God. We want a specific linking to God or Christ since this is the purpose of the text. Thus, "the celebration continued," probably would not do as a major concern: there is nothing specifically Christian in the transposition, "our celebration continues." When a text does not specifically mention God or Christ, for instance the parable of the Good Samaritan, it would be good to choose a concern whose transposition mentions God or Christ. Thus, if the major concern of the text was, "the cries of need from the ditch were answered," the major concern of the sermon/homily might be, "God hears the cries of the needy," or, "God addresses us from unlikely places."

The major concern of the text is not the text in a nutshell, but it is one route to truth. It is certainly the gospel idea that interested us most and may be a revised form of the first guess. It is one path into the text; if we follow it we will end up at the heart of the arena of authentic interpretation. And the major concern of the sermon/homily is a path that will lead the congregation to the heart of the message for today. These two paths lead us into personal confrontation with the saving message of Christ.

It may be noted that while the ideas of major concerns developed here are new to homiletics, they are not without precedent. Although there are some rather remote similarities to "transposition" in a few books (including what Fred Craddock does with theme, subject, and title[24]) the closest similarity is in *Building Sermons to Meet People's Needs* by Harold T. Bryson and James C. Taylor. Their approach to preaching is different from what is presented here, but they nonetheless employ a similar polarity between what they call the text (essence of the text in a sentence—"ETS") and the proposition (essence of the sermon in a sentence—"ESS").[25] The similarities with our "major concern of the text" and "major concern of the sermon" are superficial, however. The differences are evident in the understanding of how these arise out of the text itself; of how they function in the sermon/homily; of how they relate to other textual ideas; and of how they relate to law and gospel.

In the next chapter I will go into detail on how to select minor concerns for use in preaching, how to flesh them out, and how to choose a particular form. But now let us touch briefly on how to use the central idea. The first thing to note is that it will be the approximate structural center of the sermon or homily (even though its location may tend to vary anywhere between 60/40 and 40/60). It forms the turning point from law to gospel precisely because it is potential good news and we choose to let it bear the weight of the pivot. It is at the reversal, and only at the reversal, that we develop it, even though we may mention it at numerous other places. Thus at the reversal we might devote one substantial paragraph to developing the major concern of the text, giving relevant supporting textual and exegetical material. We would follow that by another substantial paragraph dealing with the major concern of the sermon/homily (i.e., talking about the meaning of this good-news idea for our situation).

The congregation will recognize the central idea partly because it occupies a central and dominant position in the movement of the preaching. Equally important, however, is that the congregation will recognize it because the preacher will repeat the exact wording of either the major concern of the text, or the major concern of the sermon/homily, or both, at numerous other places in the course of the preaching. The surprising thing is that this kind of repetition works; we are talking about oral delivery, and it operates on rules different from written presentation. One of my students experimented by using her central idea twelve times, and no one felt it was obvious or excessive!

In both music and dance a central theme will be introduced early, only hinting at what is to come. The same may be true for preaching. The congregation wants to know, almost from the outset, what this sermon or homily is about. However often the central idea is repeated in the course of the preaching, as a general rule it should appear early. Stated early it does not give away the plot, since it is not developed, but merely stands as a kind of signpost indicating the direction we are going. Similarly, it is a good general rule to touch on it again at the end, as a reminder of where we have been. While it will only be *developed* in the one place, that is at the reversal point, it needs to be *mentioned* a minimum of three times for us to hear it, and these strategic locations recommend themselves.

The threefold repetition fulfills the old rubric, "Say what you will say, say it, and say what you have said."

We will find that the central idea will become a listening and remembering device not just for our congregation, but for us as well. It will stand almost as a creedal or capsule statement of the sermon or homily. If the congregation remember nothing else from the preaching they should be able to state fairly clearly our central idea—whether this is our major concern of the text or our major concern of the sermon/homily will not matter since they are so closely related. It will be an idea that they can recall over the dinner table and share in their faith-witnessing throughout the week.

For now we end up with our picture looking like this:

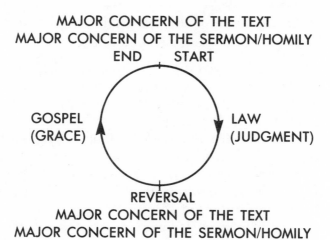

MAJOR CONCERN OF THE TEXT
MAJOR CONCERN OF THE SERMON/HOMILY
END   START

GOSPEL   LAW
(GRACE)   (JUDGMENT)

REVERSAL
MAJOR CONCERN OF THE TEXT
MAJOR CONCERN OF THE SERMON/HOMILY

Playing with the Ideas

We should never fear that we will not find water in the well of each text. What we are doing is serious, but just as David danced when the Ark was being brought into Jerusalem, we too might allow ourselves to think of our current task as involving play. If you have formed the lists for your biblical text, here are four sometimes playful ways of finding additional law and gospel concerns.

A. **Substitution.**   Most of the previous transpositions of concerns of the text were done through simple substitution of words. Just for fun, break any concern of the text into its individual words and play with substitutions for some of the words. Thus the earlier concern of the text "Jesus was at the wedding" looks like this broken up:

Jesus / was at / the wedding.

The concern of the sermon/homily became:

Jesus / is present / at our celebrations.

But what if in forming the latter we substituted "the church" or "love" or "baptism" for "Jesus" and perhaps also some other phrases for "our celebrations"? We could play with the various possibilities until one sparked for us. What about, "We are present at the celebrations of the Church," an idea we could develop to speak about the Church universal or about our participation in the communion of saints? Whenever you are doing your transpositions remember to consider such words as "baptism," "the Church," "communion," "the Holy Spirit," "the sacraments," "the Word," or "the gospel" as appropriate theological substitutions for "Jesus" or "God," substitutions that can open up new directions for our preaching and begin to hint at how any text can speak to any situation.

B. **Inversion**.   If we are short of sufficient gospel concerns, we can invert a law concern of the text into a gospel concern of the text. We then must check to see if this inverse is true of the text. Thus, "Jesus / appears / indifferent," prompted "Jesus / was not / indifferent," which was also true of the text. Inversion involves simple negation. Thus, "the celebration / was / in danger / of ending" became, "with Jesus present / the celebration / does not end." In the other direction, a gospel concern of text, "Jesus / turns / water / into / wine," can become a law concern of text, "without Jesus acting / the water / would have remained / water." Simple inversion is like flipping pancakes to see what the other side looks like.

Inversion may be used not just to create an additional concern of the text. It may also be used between a concern of the text and a concern of the sermon/homily. "Jesus / turns / water / into / wine" conceivably could be developed briefly in the law section (if we are sparse in the law section) with the main development being given to the concern of the sermon/homily, which by inversion would become, "we turn wine into water" or "we refuse to celebrate." Moving in the other direction, from law to gospel, we have the possibility of "the wine ran out" becoming "our rejoicing need not end." This can be helpful at times, but it is generally a "last ditch" device.

C. **Amplification.**   If the volume is low on the concern of the text, turn it up. Amplification refers to the process of making louder the idea that the text suggests to us. For instance, the gospel concern of text, "more guests came than expected," might become "more guests come than we expect" and could then be amplified, "God's blessings are more than we expect." While the concern of the text may have only a hint of gospel, this hint can always be amplified in the concern of the sermon/homily by introducing, as we noted above, "God," "Christ," "the Holy Spirit," "the sacraments," "the Word," "the church," "the gospel," or some such term to result in a theological statement we would affirm.

Amplification is of particular importance in preaching on Old Testament texts, a subject much too large to deal with in detail here, but the principle may be developed briefly. It is essential in dealing with Old Testament texts to treat them with the same kind of integrity within the Hebrew understanding as we bring to the New Testament texts within the Christian understanding. But as Elizabeth Achtemeier has stressed in her *The Old Testament and the Proclamation of the Gospel*,[26] we only have claim to the Old Testament through Christ. It is a common mistake when we deal with an Old Testament text to switch to the New Testament for words of hope. What we could do is listen for God's Word of hope in the earlier text and use the insights from the New Testament, only to amplify what we have already heard. For instance, Leviticus 13 deals with regulations concerning skin disease: those who are ill must be brought to the priest to be judged clean or unclean. It is the kind of passage that few of us would choose to preach, for what good news is there? But exegesis tells us that segregation of those with communicable skin disease was the only way of preserving the health of the larger community. One gospel concern of the text could be, "The law preserves the health of the community." Another could be, "The priest declared the clean to be clean." Concerning the latter, which may seem to be a weak gospel concern, we might use amplification to develop a gospel concern of the sermon/homily: "In Christ we have a priest who has declared us clean."

A second example of amplification and the Old Testament may be found in Ezekiel 18:1-9, 25-29. The ancient proverb is quoted, "The [parents] eat sour grapes, and the children's teeth are set on edge," and God says that this should no longer be quoted, for all belong to God; henceforth the one who sins shall die and a repentant sinner shall be saved. Inversion could be used to produce, "The parents eat sour grapes, and the children's teeth are not set on edge." Amplification might pick up the idea of repentance in the passage: "In Christ sinners are saved."

Amplification includes appealing to the wider context of our faith, to its doctrines and the larger Christian story. The liturgical season, which often has intimate connections with the text, can be one source of concerns for preaching. And the resurrection is always a good news concern of every text. As all preaching is Christocentric, every sermon or homily should include direct or indirect reference to the cross. But the cross should never be used as a way of avoiding the difficulties of the text at hand. Rather it should be a way of supplementing the good news we have already found in our text.

D. **A resurrection hermeneutic.**   As Christians, whenever we deal with any scriptural text, we are viewing it with the cross and resurrection in mind and hence we are always using what may be called a resurrection hermeneutic. There are times in dealing with law and gospel, judgment and grace, when it is important to use a specific form of resurrection hermeneutic to understand a particular text and to find good news. There is perhaps no better way of illustrating the overall importance of what we are trying to do with law and gospel than to take two specialized cases of this. Among the most difficult texts to preach are the gospel apocalyptic accounts of the Second Coming. They often hold particular problems for us because, if they do not contain imagery that to modern ears sounds frighteningly like nuclear annihilation, they at least contain violent unsettling images.

In Matthew 24:36-44, Jesus uses violent images to talk about God's approach: it will be as sudden as the flood in Noah's time, as unsettling as kidnappings in the field and by the handmill, and as certain as a thief will come to a careless homeowner. Theologically we would affirm that while God can use even violence for good, God never approaches us in violence. Nonetheless, our deep fear may be captured by the violent images in the text, the fear that in the Second Coming

God will reject us. Thus when we are trying to preach on a tough text like this and potential good news does not seem readily at hand, we might check to see, as is the case with this text, if the words are suggested to be pre-resurrection words from Jesus' earthly ministry. *This resurrection hermeneutic indicates that if the resurrection happened between the time Jesus uttered the words and now, their meaning may have been changed by the fact of the resurrection itself.*

This is how our text might begin to sound in the gospel section of our sermon or homily if we were preaching: "Yes, God's advent is sudden, as sudden as the flood, but we shall not be swept away. We shall be borne over the waves by God's Son. Yes, God's advent is certain, certain to come to each of us in the field or by the handmill or in the home or office, but we stand secure in Christ. And yes, God's advent steals upon us like the thief to an empty home, but God is watching over us to make sure we are not caught unaware. God is coming to us in judgment, judgment that has already been borne for us on the cross. We may put away our fear." Because of our hermeneutic, the elements of the text that struck us so forcefully as law now may begin to be bearers of grace for us. An alternate way of treating the same text would be to say, "God's advent is like the coming of a flood, but it will be a flood of grace upon the land. And it is like the coming of a kidnapper or a thief, but the thief is Christ who will steal our hearts away."

One further example may clarify matters. Frequently within texts there are individuals who seem to be outside God's grace. In our congrega-

tions there are always people who will identify
with those individuals in the texts and who will
believe that they are similarly outside God's
grace. For this reason alone it may be important
to suggest possible good news, even for the ones
who are apparently rejected. The rich man and
Lazarus is a case in point (Luke 16:19-31). After
death, when the rich man is separated from
Abraham and Lazarus by a great chasm, Abraham tells him that the chasm is fixed and that no
one can cross it. If we employ our specific
resurrection hermeneutic here, we recognize that
Jesus told this story as part of his earthly
ministry. Might the resurrection event have
altered the meaning of this text? If we imagine
that we have the text written on an overhead
projector, we are placing over it what we might
call a resurrection transparency,, and it begins to
look different. Even Abraham would not presume
to limit what God could do. We could develop the
idea that in the cross and resurrection, Christ has
bridged the chasm.

We have come to the end of a difficult chapter
on a difficult subject. What we have been talking
about is important because it is foundational to
the entire sermon or homily. But our day is
Tuesday and in terms of the actual work required,
the burden is light. The ideas we have been
working on have been relatively few: law and
gospel, determining the central idea, transposing,
and conceiving the overarching spark for the
circle. From here on our going should be easier.
We are now ready to examine how we might begin
fleshing out what we will preach.

Story and Doctrine

Some things do not change, and the need for preaching to be relevant, to reach into the life experiences of the congregation, be those experiences as mundane as the daily trip home or as poignant as the death of a loved one, remains as constant as the ticking of the town clock. Benjamin Franklin, never a regular church attender, stopped going completely because of the preaching: "Had [the minister] been, *in my opinion*, a good preacher, perhaps I might have continued . . . but his discourses were chiefly either polemic arguments or explications of the peculiar doctrines of our sect, and were all to me very dry, uninteresting and unedifying."[1] Ralph Waldo Emerson's Divinity School Address, a hundred years later, in 1838, made a similar complaint about a preacher:

143

> This man had ploughed and planted and talked and bought and sold; he had read books; he had eaten and drunken; his head aches, his heart throbs; he smiles and suffers; yet there was not a surmise, a hint, in all of the discourse, that he had ever lived at all. Not a line did he draw out of real history. The true preacher can be known by this, that he deals out to the people his life—life passed through the fire of thought.[2]

In the early 1900s, Alfred E. Garvie was instructing his lay preachers in London on the same need for relevance: "In the structure of the sermon, we must not only seek to assist the memory, but we must try also to stimulate the imagination. In order to do this we must ourselves not only conceive the truth as thought, but perceive it as life. . . . the preacher should not conceive his message as doctrine, but perceive it as experience."[3] This was arguing not for experience as a substitute for doctrine, but rather for doctrine that had the flavor of experience.

Both the need and the problem remain the same today. The problem may be much larger than our subject of preaching. For instance, William F. Lynch wrote a book on imagination two decades ago in which he instructed Christians to use what he called "analogical imagination," not to escape reality, but to perceive it. Through imagination one discerned God's presence in the midst of one's struggles: "This path . . . leads . . . through our labor, our disappointments, our friends, our game legs, our harvests, our subjection to time. . . .We must go *through* the finite, the limited, the definite, omitting none of it lest we omit some of the

potencies of being-in-the-flesh."[4] And Sallie
McFague recently challenged systematic theology (which she identifies as using "conceptual" or
"secondary religious language") not to lose touch
with the experience out of which it arises (and
which uses "imagistic" or "primary religious
language").[5] Whatever the merits of her particular argument, the issue she is raising is how our
reflections about the faith relate to Christian life.

Preaching cannot remain untouched by the
fabric of daily living. The question is how daily
life is to be incorporated. The danger in one
direction is that experience is eclipsed in the
preaching, leaving us groping in the dark for the
assistance we may need. An equal danger is that
experience will be presented in a glaring light
without the filtering lenses of biblical and
theological tradition to give us understanding.
Relevance in the pulpit is relevance to experience
and tradition.

It is imagination of the heart, imagination
leavened by scripture and experience, that can
help us make preaching relevant for today. We
have all felt the spark that can exist between
experience and doctrine. It flashes when an
experience suddenly is understood as being the
issue to which a particular Christian doctrine is
addressed: for instance to understand betrayal by
a colleague in light of the vulnerability of Christ.
It flashes also in the other direction, when a
doctrine we have been studying suddenly makes
sense in the lives around us: for instance when the
resurrection, though unique in Christ, is recognized as an event now, in the life of the woman
sitting across the coffee table from us.

How relevance in preaching is to be achieved
has received less common consent than the idea
that it should be achieved. Now, however, it is
around the issue of experience that many in
homiletics are finding general concurrence.
While narrative or story is not the only way to
convey experience in preaching, it is nonetheless
the most concrete way, and at times the most
responsible. What is currently being said belongs
to the narrative theology movement that currently is found in a variety of disciplines. Story
may not seem to be anything new to preaching:
we shall see in a moment what makes the claims
about story a departure for preaching. The
freshness of the current chapter, in addition to
this, may be found in several areas: (1) in
sketching the history of story and doctrine in
preaching, (2) in suggesting ways to employ and
balance story and doctrine better, and (3) in
suggesting ways of understanding form and
structure for preaching.

One aim of the present chapter is to suggest
how to begin fleshing out the sermon or homily.
On Monday we concentrated on the spark
between concerns of the text and concerns of the
sermon/homily. On Tuesday we struggled with
law and gospel. But both of these polarities are on
a basic structural level of homiletics. Now, on
Wednesday, we need to begin giving them shape
and substance, weight and character. Our concentration here is on the juxtaposition or spark of
experience and doctrine, which hereafter we will
refer to as story and doctrine. We may understand
these as two modes of thought, two ancient ways

of Christian expression whose tension kindles imagination of the heart.

Another aim is to try to clarify what we mean by story in homiletics since it has been batted about so much of late that it is becoming as useful as a dented table tennis ball. *We may begin by defining story as a sequence of events or images that employs plot, character, and emotion.* Plot gives it direction; character gives it humanity; and emotion gives it people in relationship. On a deeper level, story also includes intellect, intuition, and the senses. A more poetic way of defining it is to say that it is experience extracted from the dulling flow of time and held between the fingers of memory like the fractured fragments of the day. It reflects normal life in its brokenness with often embarrassing clarity. It does this because it is the way we experience everyday life. As Stephen Crites said in a seminal essay in the early 1970s, there is a "narrative quality of experience": we all experience life as a kind of story that may *seem* to have its own plot involving friendly and hostile characters, even though no plot, in the sense of fate, in fact exists.[6] Story is what happens when we teach children about Jesus; or when the pulpit's shoe-worn steps of stone are recognized as the ones that grandpa climbed; or when the Bible verse you heard so often suddenly, brilliantly, lights up the hospital room with new promise.

We may define doctrine as the statements, assertions, or teachings of the church about particular aspects of Christian faith. Doctrines are one way the church has used to reflect on the nature of God, the person of Christ, the act of

salvation, human nature, and the like. Of necessity these change and are revamped with each
successive age. Doctrine can be understood in a
wider sense, as William J. Carl III has used it in
his *Preaching Christian Doctrine* (Fortress Press,
1984), to mean anything the church teaches,
whether a particular doctrine is in mind or not, or
whether the form is one of doctrine or narrative.
Here we are staying with the narrower, more
common understanding of doctrine as propositional or abstract thought that seeks to provide
understanding of faith. This mode of expression is
sometimes characterized as linear or convergent
thought, converging on a particular point or idea,
as opposed to the non-linear, imagistic, or
divergent thought pattern of narrative that casts
a web of thoughts in a variety of directions. Some
people distinguish between doctrine and story by
using the popular but overly simplistic (from a
biological point of view) distinction between the
brain's left hemisphere (logical, informational,
sequential) and the right hemisphere (creative,
intuitive, emotional). We all have a capacity for
using both, but most of us are dominant in one.

This last point may be the strongest argument
for the need to seek a balance between story and
doctrine in our preaching, as we will argue here.
God save us in our full humanity, with minds and
bodies connected—not separated with thought
cut off from feeling, as though the ancient Greek
body-spirit distinction is Christian. It is the whole
person we are seeking to address, with each
person valued in the fullness of who God intends
that person to be. But the argument for balance
extends beyond concerns for individual whole-

ness. Preaching must value and reach out to embrace the whole body of Christ, those who respond most readily to story and those who respond most readily to doctrinal formulation. Every congregation needs both story and doctrine in order for everyone to be addressed; thus every preacher benefits from being informed by the two.

The faith community with its epistles and gospels has always been made up of "doctrine people," who are most intrigued with sound doctrinal reflection, and "story people," whose hearts and minds come alive most with a good story. In the tension between story and doctrine, faith and imagination are nourished. They are in proper relationship when they critique each other, like two lovers checking how each is dressed on the way out the door. We test our scriptural interpretations and our life experiences with doctrine. And we test our doctrines with the Bible story and the stories of our lives. When story and doctrine are split from each other in important and prolonged ways, faith and imagination will suffer. When they are together, they illuminate each other.

That is why preaching needs to balance story and doctrine. As with law and gospel, a rough fifty-fifty balance might be our normal goal. This balance enables the most frequent sparking between experience and doctrine with the richest insights into new directions for faith.

The juxtaposition of story and doctrine has not been nurtured in preaching as much as it needs to be. This is true concerning some who advocate story. They advocate that the sermon or homily should be totally story, or imply that the story is *the* message, as though doctrinal or propositional speaking and hearing no longer counts.[7] The lack of balance was also true in former years when doctrine tended to dominate, when story was understood to appeal simply to emotion and when there was little patience for extra-biblical material. It is understandable that many people are having difficulty grasping some of the recent thought about narrative in homiletics or making the practical transitions.

What is new in the current understanding about story? After all, what is more predictable in a sermon than the illustration? Can we not assume that story now is the same as story yesterday, and story tomorrow? The newness comes in our understanding of art and how art works. Art in general operates by its own rules, like a blossoming plant, to communicate the artist's ideas and feelings *and to evoke from the viewer a response.* It is a form of two-way communication since clearly it is not simply intending to convey information in the manner that a newspaper reports on the day's happenings at the legislature buildings. Artistic creation in the pulpit has been regarded with suspicion in the past and sometimes rightly so, considering what often passed for it. As Garvie said in 1906, "Sunsets, and waterfalls, and flowers, and birds, are not necessary to every sermon; still less should descriptions of scenery form the greater part of a sermon. . . . Preaching is not art or poetry, although it may use both."[8] As long as preaching is regarded as primarily a one-way event, there can be little room for the kind of art that encourages two-way communication.

Clearly there can be advantages to either approach. If you are standing on a busy express-way with a flat tire, chances are that you do not want to open the owner's manual to read a poem, however relevant it might be. For some, the primary purpose of preaching is to instruct in the faith; this dates back in part to the days in which the preacher was the most educated member of a community and was expected to use the pulpit time to educate the congregation. Illustrations were to be used "only to explain the truth or enforce the duty being taught,"[9] or, to quote some current advice, to give the congregation a "rest": "They let the congregation breathe more easily before plunging back into the thought line of the sermon."[10] The implication, of course, is that the illustration is secondary, since it is not part of the thought line and is present only to serve the doctrinal point already made. While illustration is not part of the real meat of preaching and primarily represents a concession to the salad eaters, it nonetheless serves a useful purpose in clearing the palate. To switch metaphors, the illustration is like a servant, and like the servants of former days, is never allowed a voice of its own.

By contrast an emerging understanding of preaching sees it not primarily as teaching, although this is always a part, but as an invitation to faith. The art of narrative serves this invita-tional stance by involving the listener and evoking a response. No longer do we say that story merely serves to instruct. No longer might we use a story just to get the congregation in the mood to receive a doctrinal message. No longer can we say that we make our doctrinal point and illustrate it with a story. No longer can we speak of doctrine as *the meaning* and story as *the practice* or of doctrine as primary and story as secondary. McLuhan's statement that "the medium is the message" was not far off the mark. It is not that the story is the message, but that the story is the story's message. The story makes its own point. The story is the point.

According to the New Testament, Jesus didn't spend much time preaching doctrine, but he did tell a lot of stories. Like the parables, the point a story makes may be understood in a variety of ways, for it in fact makes many points. To a certain extent this richness of meaning is allowed to stand: the story is not reduced to a moral the way a flower may be stripped of all its petals leaving just the center. Rather the blossom is valued in its own right and is simply woven into the fabric of the preaching in such a way that its location there seems essential to the design and texture of the whole.

The quiet revolution going on in the last two decades in relation to story demands that story and doctrine be valued as having equal importance for preaching. Most revolutions in their early phases are misinterpreted as a minority expression, a passing fad soon to go the way of the hula hoop and the pet rock. Story too is currently dismissed as a fad by some, sometimes by the same ones who say that nothing has changed. More distressing is the fact that even well-respected scholars have occasionally misread the signs. James Breech, whose *The Silence of Jesus* makes an important contribution to understanding Jesus as a storyteller, concludes that Jesus told no stories about himself and therefore contrasts "most contemporary storytellers" who tell stories about themselves and thereby serve their own ego needs.[11] William H. Willimon similarly reduces the narrative movement to egocentrism. In a review of narrative and preaching (as he finds it in Frederick Buechner, Fred Craddock, and Tom Troeger), he concludes that, "the effort to reduce preaching to the narrative of *my* story claims too much for our stories and too little for the biblical story."[12] The analysis would benefit from wider perusal of books such as Robert P. Waznak's *Sunday After Sunday* which make it clear that, at a minimum, the emphasis is on three stories: the story of God, the story of the preacher, and the story of the listener.[13]

The purpose of the current writing is to give the biblical text the centrality it must have. But Willimon is right in warning that story is no panacea—"stories are susceptible to the same self-serving falsehood and delusion as any other creative human activity." The thrust today must be to resist any supremacy of story *over* doctrine, and rather to affirm their *equal* status as different but related ways of communicating the faith.

A Brief History of Story and Doctrine for Preaching

Reestablishing mutuality between story and doctrine will be a long-term task for the church. There is a long bias in Christian history that goes against it and that is important for us to understand. Given the importance of narrative today, it is somewhat surprising that even a brief history of story and doctrine for preaching, as will be sketched here, has not been done.

For a variety of reasons the church over the ages has been less trustful of story than it has been of doctrine. One of the current claims about story is that it is one essential way of doing theology. But this new claim in our time is in fact an ancient practice of the church. The church from the time of Paul has had a tradition of doctrinal thought, but for the first two centuries this is balanced by its rich tradition of story. Story is not separate from theology, or rather, story is seen as a primary vehicle for communicating the Christian message. The footprints of story make at least as deep an impression in the sand of the early church as the footprints of doctrine.

This is readily seen if we look beyond the books of our New Testament, for instance to the apocrypha of the New Testament; there are many gospels, books of acts, epistles, and books of revelation written in the first two centuries and used widely in the church as devotional and liturgical reading. Many focus on the role of women in the ministry of the early church (i.e., the Acts of Peter recounts stories of Peter's daughter and the daughter of the gardener; the Acts of Paul tells of a woman preacher originally converted by Paul), which is one reason feminist theology is interested in their exclusion from the canon; and many retell Jesus' life or sayings (i.e., Tatian's *Diatessaron* combines and harmonizes our four Gospels; the Gospel of the Hebrews, which originated in Egypt, bears little resemblance to our Gospels).[14] These flourish without the church ever thinking of establishing a distinct new canon through selection of only the best books available.

This early Christian literature takes a variety of forms but we may classify much of it as story and much as doctrine. This should be no surprise since the Jewish faith out of which Christianity grew was (and still is) more rooted in story than in doctrine. Stories were seen as an effective way of communicating theological truths and the Synoptic Gospels, which by the time of Justin Martyr in A.D. 165 were being regarded as of primary importance, were part of this large story tradition. Similarly the epistles were regarded as primary and a part of the large doctrinal tradition.

It is around the third century that something fascinating happens. Up to this period of the church's life, story and doctrine show a remarkable balance. Then, suddenly, the situation changes in a radical way: the footprints of story are faint and almost disappear while those of doctrine are more clearly defined. Why is it that from the fourth century to the present, narrative has been almost excluded from theology? What happened to make story often regarded as inferior to doctrine? Why today does our word "theology" still imply doctrine and not story? Why today does our word "theologian" generally imply the person who teaches in a seminary and not also the person in the parish who preaches or teaches the faith?

We will mention only four related answers here. The first is that narrative tended to become identified with heretical Gnosticism. Marcion's Gnostic canon excluded all of our Gospels (except for Marcion's edited version of Luke), and it also indirectly encouraged the writing of many additional gospels and epistles for worship and devotional use. But his canon, which was kept open, prompted in response a closed canon within orthodox Christianity by the Council of Hippo in 393. Canon formation helped mark the demise of narrative and encourage identification of story with heresy.

A second factor contributing to the death of narrative was the desire of early Christian Platonists such as Clement and Origen to introduce philosophy to Christianity, a move that served to shift Christianity from its identification as a Jewish sect to a religion more acceptable for Roman pagans. Christians appealed to Plato for proof of God and for evidence of everything from Logos to the immortality of the soul.

Third, Christianity became the religion of the state. If the church was to retain its state privilege it could no longer be a revolutionary force. Individuals and communities could not be prophetic in a manner that would threaten the church at large; prophecy was to be left to the hierarchy of the church. This movement to orthodoxy and central power sought to suppress all forms of schismatic expression, narrative and otherwise. Doctrine was a saving force for the church and it also became its chief weapon against heresy. Doctrinal thought (of the right kind) became identified with orthodoxy.

Finally, when martyrdom was no longer something to which devout Christians might aspire, stories of martyrdom became replaced by stories of spiritual martyrdom; thus, an entire genre of

Christian stories were diluted in impact and importance.[15]

With the exceptions of Augustine's *Confessions* (397) and the writings of the mystics, story in general did not survive in the mainstream of theology. The stories of canonized Scriptures were appreciated, as indicated in the growth of exegetical study and in the identification of the fourfold "levels of interpretation" which were developed from Origen and Augustine onward: literal, allegorical, anagogical, and tropological. But church fathers writing about story was not the same thing as writing story. Moreover, determining the correct meanings of story became a way of policing the stories to ensure that they were interpreted safely and correctly. The route that the church took, and has consistently taken according to Hans Frei, was to turn story into philosophy, thereby ascribing meaning to story rather than allowing story to stand on its own to be evaluated by the experience of the hearer or reader.[16]

Further evidence of the church's historic mistrust of story was its role in the death of Roman drama, which it opposed on a variety of grounds including its associations with paganism, its ridicule of Christianity, and the immorality of the players. For five hundred years from the decline of the Roman Empire there was no significant dramatic tradition in the West.[17] When it reappeared it was not a continuation of the tradition of Roman drama but rather a separate tradition emerging from the liturgy and teachings of the church.

The one place where story may be said to have

survived, although severely muzzled and its impact carefully restrained, was in the pulpit. A classical understanding of narrative in preaching is evident throughout history. Stories took the form of examples, illustrations, and anecdotes. Scriptural narratives were expounded. Story was subservient to doctrine. Every story served a point. These preachers, like us, often confused enabling faith (opening responsible decisions for people) with moralizing (telling people what they must do). Often, however, it was the kind of stories that were used that posed the problem, a problem that Robert Waznak says neither the Protestant nor Catholic Reformation resolved:

> The Reformers were appalled by many of the sermons of their day which were filled with anecdotes about animals, the Crusades, and exaggerated tales of the saints, but had little to do with the Gospel. It was unfortunate, however, that in many of the sermons of the early Reformers, story simply was substituted for dry theological argument. The preaching in the Catholic Church following the Council of Trent was no better. Here, too, story was often lost to a colorless exposition of Catholic doctrine."[18]

Why in our own time is story being reassessed for theological purposes? Here are a number of important reasons we may list:

1. Pursuit of the "historical Jesus" combined with New Testament structuralist studies have led to a new appreciation of the role of parable in Jesus' own teaching. This in turn has led to an increased awareness of story as the primary level by which people enter the Christian faith and are sustained in it.

2. Recognition of the importance of story is not an isolated phenomenon. It is affirmed in homiletics, Christian ethics, New Testament, comparative religion, in black, liberation, and feminist theologies, in psychotherapy and psychiatry,[19] and in the holistic health movement.

3. Increased interest in salvation history *(heilsgeschichte)*, in God's saving acts through history, has led many to criticize traditional theology for not taking history seriously, for ignoring suffering and oppression through the ages.[20] As a result there is new value placed on stories of particular groups in society that have previously been ignored or marginalized.

4. There is new interest in myth arising out of the work of such individuals as John Paul Sartre, Paul Ricoeur, and Roland Barthes. We are now discovering that it is important for us to hear stories from all cultures and religions as a way of enabling us better to understand our own.[21]

5. The impact of educational theorist of the fifties and sixties (writers such as Paul Goodman, Paulo Freire, and Edgar Friedenberg) is now being felt. They stressed the need for learning to be participatory. Theory about how story communicates stresses the manner in which it is participatory, making its own point through involving the reader.

There are several reasons we can discern for the rise in importance of story today, but *fundamental to all of these is a revaluing of experience and the role of experience for the social and academic enterprise.* Narrative theology and preaching have a common goal: to pay attention to the stories at the base of Christian communities, both the biblical stories and the contemporary ones with which they intersect. If doctrine loses touch with the primary level of Christian experience it is serving no one. And if preaching values story to the extent that there is no appreciation for doctrine it too loses its purpose.

Sharing Our Stories and Doctrines

We are perhaps now moving into an era in which story and doctrine can be valued equally. In terms of our parish ministry, our day of the week is Wednesday. For the spark of imagination of the heart to occur between these important poles in our preaching, there are several things to remember as we go through the day's activities.

First, we may remember that stories are our normal way of relating our experiences and doctrines are our normal way of questioning those experiences from a faith perspective. Often what prevents us from using each more effectively is an overly elevated notion of them. We may need to change our ideas of what a story is. With story we may say, "It must be funny," "It must be complete," or "It must sound like it came from a book." Discard these ideas. There are stories all around us if we will only recognize them. Some are complete, some are incomplete. Some are funny, some are sad. They are the "stuff" of our experience—the events around the gasp or the wail; around the grinding teeth or the tingling skin; or around the trembling fingers or the clapping palms. Stories are in the words of the next telephone call, in the events behind the letter on the desk, in the newspaper, or on television, in every book we pick up and in every meeting. Many of us may not have thought of our normal discourse as story, or that story is a natural medium for us all. But when we chat over the garden fence or in the produce section of the supermarket, we are telling stories. When we tell the doctor what is wrong or tell the mechanic about the breakdown of the car, we tell stories. When we visit in parishioners' homes or in the hospital, we listen to and tell stories. Everywhere there are stories.

I often advise my students to make sure they travel the subway at rush hour (not that they often have much choice) because it is then, with people crowded into a tight space, that stories always happen. Pay attention to feelings: if something delights or bothers you, a story is there—the car breaking down can become more tolerable if we step back from ourselves and watch the story unfolding. Try telling an event from the perspective of another person, or try breaking down an event into something like our concerns of the text, and the stories will start to appear. Much may be said for good filing of stories—and most of it has been said too often for those whose files still do not work for them—but not enough has been said about the need for good listening and seeing. So much happens in one week that we need never run out of stories to tell if we teach ourselves to recognize a story when it happens. Everywhere you go simply say to yourself, "There is a story in this." *Unless we consciously remind ourselves that what we are experiencing is a story, it will slip downstream past us.* Like a person with a camera looking for a good

picture, you will start to see the stories around
you.

Similarly with doctrine our ideas may be too
lofty. Many people unfortunately think that
doctrine is abstract and remote, that its language
must be thick and heavy. To the contrary, there
should be no seams in our language between
doctrinal reflection and narrative reflection: the
two should flow easily together, as Alfred Garvie
suggested when he said that doctrine should be
conceived as experience.

Other people hear the word doctrine and think
they must try to quote or paraphrase what others
have written: there are merits in doing just that.
But it may be more helpful for us to recognize that
when we are reflecting on the faith, trying to make
sense of it in relation to experience, we are
already formulating doctrine. Doctrine is not
something fixed and rigid, which must always
remain the same, with only slight substitutions
here or there of a particular word, image, or idea
to make it contemporary. Rather, doctrine is
fluid, with set standards, to be sure, but standards
that provide room for movement and incorpora-
tion of new experience. William J. Carl's book
Doctrinal Preaching goes a long way toward
establishing this fluidity. But he does more than
this by showing that doctrinal questions arise in
every biblical text; in the sacraments, seasons,
and creeds of the church; and in the variety of
cultural contexts we find ourselves. In short,
doctrinal issues for preaching are as plenteous as
the stories that surround us.

A Wednesday night Bible study in which the
pastor acts primarily as a listener and resource

person can be an important aid in gleaning stories and doctrinal concerns from our people. Its organization might be similar to our method to this point: an opening in which the participants have the opportunity to share issues or stories with which they have been dealing; a reading of the biblical text and telling its story; an exegetical period in which the text's meaning in its own time is imagined and supplemented by our own study; and, perhaps after a break, a focusing on what it means for today, bringing in some of the stories and issues raised at the beginning.

Second, a good starting point for using both story and doctrine is to pay attention to individual words. One word can be a story. We said that a story involves plot, character, and emotion, and obviously one word cannot do that. But what happens with individual words is that the story is evoked from us. The plot, characters, and emotions are within us. Take the word "raspberry," "murky," or "handrailing." As soon as we start meditating on one of these words a story comes to mind. *A one-word story is a word about which we want to hear more.* It intrigues us, catches our attention, and begins to involve us. Listen to words. Play with them. Carry them around. Wear them. Get to know what they feel like. Know which words sound to you like a fingernail on a blackboard. Read the dictionary. Words are our tools and the more we use them the better they work for us. Words have life. We want to train ourselves to be sensitive to the dance of words, to hear their slippers squeak with their whirl and pivot. Words taste and smell, they have texture, color, and sound. They are short and tall, wide and narrow, some walk with a limp while others race along. Some words are lethargic and lazy while others are energetic and trim. In short, words are our friends. As preachers and teachers we have it incumbent upon us to get to know them, to allow them to minister to us and to use them with care in our ministry to others. It might be a good practice to find out the favorite one-word-stories of parishioners as a way of becoming conscious of the power of words for our people.

Sensitivity to individual words is as important for doctrine as it is for story. Obviously individual words represent certain doctrines: such words as "sin," "redemption," "resurrection," "baptism," and "creation." And equally obvious is that part of the interest for our people in listening to even the most difficult of ideas explained, can be the words we choose to make the doctrine come alive. There is no substitute for a good use of the language. Less obvious may be the way in which some words imply certain doctrines: thus "wrong," "death," or "chaos" might suggest the doctrine of sin or evil; and "love," "fullness," or "unity" might suggest the doctrine of marriage or of God's act of reconciliation.

Third, avoid abstract words wherever possible when dealing with doctrine or story. Most abstract words have lost the polarity or tension they had at one stage, as we discussed in chapter 1. This caution applies to many of our doctrinal words, our standard religious phrases, and our religious jargon. Such words as "incarnation," "atone-ment," "salvation," as we said, must not be discarded, but should be given renewed meaning in part through careful use. Other words to use sparingly are the abstract words "love," "anger," and "beautiful," which are like quarters that have been spent so often we no longer see the face on the coin. Whenever we are tempted to use an abstract word in preaching, we should at least ask ourselves if a specific instance would not work better. As a way of avoiding an abstract word in preaching we may wish we had a good story to tell, but it is good to remember that a catalog of images can be just as effective. The principle here is, "Don't explain what it is, show us what it is." For instance, what does love look like? Where have we seen it? Was it in the gentleness of the child's touch, or in the eyes as they followed the partner across the lawn, or in the greeting card that was left on the table? Catalogs of images (like the one just used) help listeners remember their own stories and help convince them that the speaker is addressing reality.

A fourth point is to pay attention to detail, being exact but not exacting. Doctrinal reflection needs to be clear but not laborious. There are few things more distracting and annoying in a sermon than either an overly long argument or a heavily descriptive passage that seems to relate to nothing. Stories too should be slim—never larded with detail. We may not use a lot of details in a story, yet to tell a story well, indeed to talk about a biblical story well, we must know details the hearer may never know.

Virginia Woolf gave excellent advice. A guest wanted to know how to write a story and Woolf answered by asking the guest for all the details about waking that morning. What woke you?

Were the birds singing? Was the window open? Were you warm? What did you feel? We edit out many of these details from our normal experience before they even awaken in our minds, but we need to know them to tell a story well. The same is true for doctrine, we need to know the complexity of thought behind an idea in order to be able to present it with simplicity. An excellent way for the preacher to develop narrative and doctrinal skills is to try thoughts on parishioners before Sunday. A good story is always worth retelling. Children's stories should be tested with children if possible, and doctrinal reflection only improves with conversation about doctrine.

Fifth, finding stories or choosing doctrines for preaching is a technical skill of "imagination of the heart" which can help avoid writer's "block." It is with the ideas of (a) one-word stories and (b) words leading to doctrines that we may find a way around writer's "block." Recall that when we spoke of transposing concerns of the text we spoke of circling or highlighting particular words or word-groupings and of free-associating until we came up with a concern of the sermon/homily that interested us. We have already developed several text-situation juxtapositions or units (a concern of the text plus a concern of the sermon/homily). We may go to them and again circle words for free-association, this time with the purpose of locating specific stories and doctrines.

An approach that may be helpful is to use the concerns of the text to locate relevant doctrines and the concerns of the sermon/homily to evoke relevant stories or experiences. The major concern of the text and the major concern of the sermon/homily will obviously be the most important in this process. In this way the spark between story and doctrine will reinforce the spark between the biblical text and our situation. But this is only a suggestion and the reader may find other ways to go. Let us see what this would look like, however.

If we want to identify relevant doctrinal issues, take some concerns of the text and circle or highlight the key words. The major concern of the text will be most important to do this with since it is the central textual idea we will be developing. The following concerns of the texts (taken from a variety of texts) might eventually suggest the following doctrines:

SELECTING DOCTRINES

CONCERNS OF THE TEXTS		POSSIBLE DOCTRINES
Jesus / healed / the blind man.		
commanded	chaos	history
made whole	without light	creation
God acting	darkness	authority
	creation	
Jesus / turned / water / into wine.		
changed	world fullness	church
miracle	church	salvation
	communion	sacraments
	salvation	
Jesus / overturned / the temple tables.		
rules over	money-lending	judgment
confronted	disobedience	ministry
	sin	sin
		rule of Christ

It might be useful for each of us to draw up a list of the doctrines we would like to cover in the course of a year's preaching and to keep that list handy when choosing doctrines for preaching.

Let us turn now to finding stories from concerns of the sermon/homily. Most of us, when put on the spot and asked to tell a story, go blank. Yet if someone tells a story we often have no difficulty in coming up with an experience we had. We have the stories inside us, it is a matter of drawing them out. The imagination often works best if it is allowed to work at a subconscious level, that is, it is allowed time to brood over the material it has received. It also works best if the rigid linear ways of our thinking are interrupted so that other ways of thought may occur. Free-association is one way of breaking linear thought. Instead of becoming blocked when we have to think of a story, we may relax in our study and allow the stories to be evoked from us. That is one of the exciting things about drawing up concerns of the sermon/homily—the individual words will help us recall stories that we can make relevant to the text if we trust them. Draw circles around or highlight the individual words in the concerns of the sermon/homily and free-associate. Jot down individual words (one-word stories) that come to mind.

A recent book on creative writing supports what we have been saying about the need to free-associate as a way of avoiding writer's block. Composing by making a list of points we want to cover can interfere with creativity, says Gabriele Rico.[22] In her *Writing the Natural Way*, she suggests that when starting to write, people put down one word or group of words at the center of the page and draw a circle around it. The free-association that follows, she suggests, should result in each related word or thought being placed in a separate circle adjacent to the first. We end up with what she calls a "clustering" of ideas around the central one. The free-associating should continue for several minutes, she says, until we experience a shift of thought and know what we want to say, at which point we should begin writing the section on which we are working. The writing block has been bypassed. The purpose is not to try to use each circled idea, but is rather to set the creative process in motion using only those ideas that naturally flow into and from the writing.

Whether we adopt Rico's idea of clustering or not, it is essential for imagination that we allow the free-association process to take place in recovering story for preaching. With concerns of the sermon/homily we will again circle or highlight significant words (as we did in transposing) but with the sole intent this time of evoking stories from us. In the next chapter we will have more to say on the appropriate use of our stories in dealing with issues.

SELECTING STORIES

Concern of the Sermon/Homily			Possible Stories
Jesus/gives us/	newness/	of life.	
gift	fresh	hope	whatever
shares	newborn	stories	stories are
present	unsullied	faith	evoked from
free	blossoming		us by these
			words

Although we have been suggesting that doctrine be drawn from concerns of the text and that stories be drawn from concerns of the sermon/homily, we need to emphasize these are guidelines only. *When developing concerns in the sermon or homily itself, doctrine and story are equally appropriate.*

Homiletical Form, Flow, and Music

The challenge of establishing the equality of story and doctrine for preaching partly lies with homiletical structure and form. If story is to be valued alongside doctrine, it can no longer be made constantly subservient to doctrine in the organization of the sermon/homily. The familiar idea of a sermon outline that identifies key points, subpoints, and their illustrations represents a doctrine-centered approach. Logical order of points is primary. Stories of necessity are "slotted in" to assist the development of a point, but never to make a point in their own right or to have doctrine serve the story. We need, as an alternate to this, another more flexible understanding of structure and form that does not have the rigid, linear, or mechanical implications often implied by a doctrine-centered approach. We need an approach that centers on doctrine and story.

Perhaps even the idea of a sermon outline is so connected to linear thought that it should be left aside. It suggests that homiletical structure is static and that preaching is built or constructed, like so many bricks that fit neatly together in pre-determined ways, each one resting on the ones beneath it. One problem with building a sermon or homily this way is that if one brick crumbles, the rest can come falling down: if one of the preacher's premises is disputed, the entire event of preaching may be discarded. We want an idea of form with the dual values of both story and doctrine. We want something that will encourage us to think of the sermon or homily as growing, organic, or living, as having movement and rhythm. We want a notion of structure that has elasticity and flexibility. To talk about the flow may be better than to speak of an outline. We should be thinking of a river current, or of a conversation flowing, or of ideas and emotions joining together.

What we mean by flow refers to form, but let us be careful not to use the idea of form to deny, as has sometimes been the case in the past, that in preaching, form and meaning are related. Preaching that is primarily structured, Sunday after Sunday, to demonstrate rhetorical skill inevitably says something additional to the intended content: it may say that the model for ministry is one with the preacher at the center of congregational life. There are other ways in which form provides content:

> Ministers who, week after week, frame their sermons as arguments, syllogisms armed for debate, tend to give that form to the faith perspective of regular listeners. Being a Christian is proving you are right. . . . Sermons which invariably place before the congregation the "either/or" format as the way to see the issues before them contribute to oversimplification, inflexibility, and the notion that faith is always an urgent decision. In contrast "both/and"

> sermons tend to broaden horizons and sym-
> pathies but never confront the listener with a
> crisp decision. Form is so extremely important.
> Regardless of the subjects being treated, a
> preacher can thereby nourish rigidity or open-
> ness, legalism or graciousness, inclusiveness or
> exclusiveness, adversarial or conciliating men-
> tality, willingness to discuss or demand for
> immediate answers.[23]

Content is discovered in part by following the
form and form is discovered in part by following
the content. Poets since the Romantics have
known this. It was for this reason that Archibald
MacLeish said, "A poem should not mean but be,"
and we might echo, "Preaching should not mean
but be." Preaching is not just information, it is an
event. Each sermon or homily may have its own
unique form, reflecting the uniqueness of each
encounter with God's Word. To some extent this
form will be suggested by the form of the text. Not
that preaching on an epistle needs to take the
form of an epistle or that preaching on a psalm
must be a psalm. But the flavor and texture of the
scripture we preach should come through in the
preaching. We do not want to be who Craddock
warns against: "The minister [who] boils all the
water off and then preaches the stain in the
bottom of the cup."[24]

The sermon or homily will begin to write itself
if we use the imagination. This cannot be said too
often. If we listen to the biblical text it will open a
variety of rich meanings to us, will tell us what
situations to address, which stories to use, and
what doctrines we might develop. By today,
Wednesday, we have our law and gospel concerns

and now it is time for us to choose which ones we want to use and to determine their tentative order. We want to sketch the flow of the sermon. Then we can allow the text to select the stories and doctrines.

In the last chapter we made a start toward structure when we visualized the overall shape of preaching to be circular (not that our argument will be circular!). This circle in some ways will mirror the route of the hermeneutical circle we took to understand the biblical text and may in some ways suggest the circular route to understanding the congregation will take in arriving at our understanding. We start by briefly identifying our major concern of the text and/or major concern of the sermon/homily, move through the law to the heart of the good news (i.e., the reversal, which is the detailed development of the major concern of the text and the detailed development of the major concern of the sermon/ homily), and then back through gospel to a new understanding of the world under Christ and a concluding statement of the major concern of the text and/or the major concern of the sermon/ homily.

As an image of form, the circle is flawed. We noted that the hermeneutical circle is more accurately a spiral, since we do not return to the same place. There has been considerable movement and growth between our first encounter with the text and our final understanding, or between the beginning of the sermon or homily and the end. Further, we move into and out of any text several times in trying to understand it: there is a continual shifting of gravity between reader and text. The same may be true of the preaching event as well.

For our purposes of visualizing the flow, we would perhaps be better off to imagine a combination of circle and spiral, adopting one without discarding the other. If a biblical sermon or homily moves only once into the text and out of it, the circle as we have it is appropriate. But more frequently the image of biblical preaching will be a circular spiral: we spiral in and out of the text as we preach. If we conceive of each loop of the spiral being one movement into the text and then back into our situation, we can recognize that each loop represents one text-situation unit. The number of loops will vary from text to text, but a sermon or homily might look something like this:

Abbreviations: **MT/MS** = major concern of the text/ major concern of the sermon homily

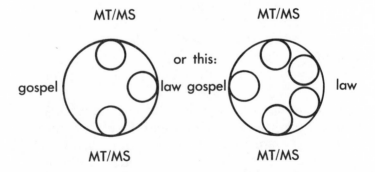

There are any number of other possible variations. Try varying the number of loops yourself. Each loop constitutes a development of a concern of the text and a development of a concern of the sermon/homily. *The major concern is always a*

*good news concern and remains the same through-
out the entire sermon or homily. All other concerns
of the text and concerns of the sermon/homily are,
by default, minor concerns, whether they are law
(law concerns by definition are minor since the
major concern is always gospel) or gospel.*

What we have here is a basic picture, with some
possible variations, for the flow of any biblical
sermon or homily. Any biblical preaching will
combine the biblical text and our situation,
whether it is done in the way we have been
suggesting with equal balance to each, or not. *To
understand the structure of any biblical preaching we
hear, all we need to remember is that any movement
into the biblical text and out of it represents a loop.
For an upward movement and completion of the
"circling spiral" there needs to be a substantial
development of gospel.* Even as some of the other
ideas we have discussed here represent certain
universal principles in homiletics, the idea of loops
for discussing structure has universal relevance.

Examining other sermons in this light is a good
way to discover further variations to the ones
suggested here. For example, I heard a sermon by
Charles L. Rice in which there were rich textual
references and images, too many to count, each of
which might form a small loop: the structure was
like a loose coil of unraveling yarn that passed
among the people, touching each one. I heard
another by Fred B. Craddock in which he simply
told five different stories of five different encoun-
ters he had had with his text (five loops). I heard
another by Charles G. Adams of Hartford Baptist
Church in Detroit in which he preached for
forty-five minutes and brought the congregation

to three distinct and mounting crescendos, each one starting slowly and moving with increasing tempo. His sermon I would understand as three circular spirals (each had the possibility of standing as a short sermon on its own) linked to one another.

We have all heard or read biblical sermons and homilies that present further variations. What is important is not that we identify each possibility here, but rather that we have the language, imagery, and theological basis for understanding, discussing, and evaluating preaching. Furthermore, it is important that we remember that what we are currently doing is establishing basic guidelines that, for a variety of legitimate reasons, might be altered. They are, at minimum, a departure place for us.

We were saying that the number of loops in our own preaching will vary according to the number of text-situation units that are developed. The amount of time devoted to different loops will also vary, still keeping in mind the overall balance of law and gospel. We may recognize that we are dealing with matters that are normally considered as musical matters: beat, rhythm, tempo, and the like.

Music in preaching is a deep area of homiletics which needs much more study than can be given here. H. Grady Davis, Charles L. Bartow, and Tom Troeger, among others, have spoken of writing for the ear, choosing musical words and varying sentence structure and length, and about cadence, pitch, and timing in delivery.[25]

Henry H. Mitchell and Bruce A. Rosenburg get closer to what I am talking about here, and not surprisingly, for they are both talking about black preaching and an oral tradition.[26] Black preaching, old Welsh preaching, indeed all folk preaching has a kind of music built into it. When Charles G. Adams in Detroit reaches one of his crescendos, the long sentences will be broken down into shorter phrases of a few syllables each and they will come with a regularity of beat that compels the listener.

In a presentation to the North American Academy of Homiletics in Toronto in 1983, Professor Gwyn Walters demonstrated from his research and his intimacy with the Welsh language what the famous old Welsh preachers in Wales sounded like in Welsh; these preachers developed their own personal tune in their preaching that in turn helped them project their voice to be heard by the thousands who would gather for outdoor preaching. Some of these tunes, he says, were written down and became some of the fine Welsh tunes we have for Christian hymns. There is music inherent in the structure of our preaching, and we might all learn to be more attentive to it.

At the simplest level of homiletical structure, each loop constitutes a beat. A homily with many loops in the law section and few loops, or perhaps just one, in the gospel section is a homily that would probably have a fast tempo in the first half and a slow, peaceful one in the second. Its music might mirror the action of a biblical text, as in the healing of Lazarus, which clearly moves from despair to peace. Or the music might simply create a mood to complement our message. Many loops, like fast music, demand much attention. Fewer loops, like slow music, can be more soothing. Preaching that ends with a fast tempo can effectively carry people out into the world to its beat: it says we have something here that matters. A sermon that ends with stillness can say something else: it says that our faith is trust-worthy, a worthy support in times of trouble.

As preachers it is important that we be aware of all the various ways in which we communicate in our preaching. Preachers today who have an aptitude for music and theory might pay particu-lar attention to thinking of sermonic structure and delivery as music.

The flow of next Sunday's preaching can be sketched quickly, perhaps between hospital visits or in a meeting (when we might be wishing we were somewhere else!). The order of our material may have some relationship to the actual chro-nology of the text, particularly at the beginning when the congregation needs to be reminded of what was in the text and the beginning of the text may be important to mention. We do not assume that our people have actually heard and absorbed the text even though it has already been read once in the service: let us think that they have only half heard it and make sure that we give them the reminders they will need to recall the rest. *But chronology of the text need rarely be our determining guide in selecting the entire chronology of the sermon or homily.* The congregation can hold the various elements of the biblical text in their minds without having to be taken back through the exact sequence of events or ideas. This is particularly important since not all Bible texts clearly move from law to gospel in the manner that we are suggesting our preaching should.

Charting the flow on a piece of paper may be done in circle or spiral form, or as an alternative, we may keep the circular flow in mind and for convenience move to a vertical charting. Each of us will find our own way of sketching it.

The following are just two possible ways in which a sermon or homily might flow. There are many others. The one on the left is what we will call *the one loop or one circle format which is ideal for short sermons or homilies on the occasion of a wedding, a funeral, the celebration of the eucharist, or a children's sermon.*[27] I sometimes wonder if this might not be a better approach than what we often practice as "the children's story." The "flow" on the right is for the "spiral" variety: it could be expanded, of course, by the addition of loops in either the law or gospel sections. The major concern of the text and major concern of the sermon/homily remain the same throughout: they do not change, it is the treatment of them in each location that varies. The minor concerns do change, however, and are used only once.

Abbreviations: **T** = concern of the text; **S** = concern of the sermon/homily **MT** = major concern of the text; **MS** = major concern of the sermon/homily

A: ONE LOOP	B: SPIRAL OR MANY LOOPS
LAW:	LAW:
MT/MS—By "inversion." This introduction could be a story or doctrine that raises the law side of the **MT/MS.**	**MT/MS**—Introduction. This could be as in "A"; or it could be just a direct statement of each—"our text today tells us that

GOSPEL:

MT—reversal. In this "one loop" format the reversal may come as early as one-third of the way through the preaching. It includes detailed treatment of the text showing how this good-news idea arises from the text.

MS: In this "one loop" format this might well include treatment of a specific theological doctrine (i.e., forgiveness). Together, the MT/MS might be occupying roughly the middle third of the loop.

MT/MS—conclusion. This again might be a story that clearly embodies the good news of the text and invites us to act in its light.

(MT) . . . and we will see that for us it means **(MS)** . . . "; or it could be a short treatment of just one.

T: A detailed treatment of an initial concern of text will help remind us of the text.

S: This shows us what the law from the text looks like in our situation.

T: A new idea, developed as above.

S: Developed as above.

GOSPEL:

MT—reversal. This gives the textual and exegetical details to support the MT as an authentic concern of the text.

MS: This begins to give us an idea of what the good news might look like in our situation.

T: A further gospel idea supported by textual data.

S: Another dimension of the text's good news for us, further opening us to acting in faith.

MT/MS—conclusion. Just a reminder of where we have been or a story that may be the flip side of the sermon's introduction.

The kinds of form we are sketching here are not rigid formulae we will follow in writing. Even in the writing process we will want to retain flexibility, even to the point of moving in quite a different direction, if the need arises. But generally this early arrangement may be expected to resemble closely the flow of the final product.

Most of us carefully avoid discipline. It seems too much like work or seems like too much work. With preaching we might not take the small amount of time needed to sketch our direction; we may instead rush right into the writing. In both my own experience and that of my students, I have found that five minutes of disciplined work can save as much as an hour or two of writing that goes astray. With the general direction firmly in mind when we start, the imagination is freed to concentrate on what it needs to focus on while we are writing.

Giving Flesh to the Form

Now that we have the form in mind we can turn our attention to fleshing out the various ideas at hand. Here are ten important guidelines, some new and some in review, to assist us.

1. The purpose of writing out the flow, in addition to helping plot where we are hoping to go, is to provide an early check for imagination. It is when we see the sermon or homily in skeletal form that we will spot whether our transpositions are as strong as they might be, whether there is sufficient textual variety among them, whether structures enabling law and gospel are present, and whether story and doctrine are likely to be balanced. It is this structure that will have to bear the weight of what we put on it; if there is a flaw apparent here, it will surely be apparent in the final product.

2. In your final sketch of the flow of your sermon/homily, choose concerns of the text that are different from one another. This will add variety. Even more important, when you later develop these concerns with supporting details from the text and exegetical sources, you will not be drawing on the same material each time. *The final selection of which text-situation units to include should also consider variety in the transpositions.* With concerns of the sermon/homily, it is wise to alternate focus between transpositions that focus on those of us in the church and transpositions that focus on issues for the broader fabric of human life in the world. Thus a transposition that reads "we (in the church) must be righteous," could be transposed a second time to provide us with a broader focus than just the church: "the world places burdens on us." Continual focus on the church alone narrows our vision and will soon make us (and our congregations) bored with our own preaching.

3. Choose your final concerns because of their inherent interest to you. You do not need to select gospel concerns in relation to law concerns; in other words they do not need to match. Only after you have chosen your concerns of the text and their transpositions into concerns of the sermon/ homily, do you need to consider what you might

say or which stories or doctrines you might imply.
These basic structural units for the preaching will
provide plenty of sparks. I have seen students
subvert the transposition process by conceiving
first of what they want to preach and then by
trying to do transpositions that will enable this.
Forcing concerns of the sermon/homily in this
manner is unnecessary. It comes from anxiety
over what will be the final product. Simply do one
step at a time. The ideas that you want to include
will be able to be woven into the development of
the concerns that you choose. The choice of these
concerns simply will provide a structure for your
message. Their selection does not exclude material so much as it will provide the means by
which you may say it. The structure will give your
preaching coherence and unity. The unity will not
be the linear unity of a lecture or of an argument
in a debate, for that is not what we are after.
Rather, the unity is the kind we find in most
conversations: subjects change easily from one to
another, yet generally within a limited range and
with a specific overall thrust.

4. *Let the concerns of the text and concerns of the
sermon/homily dictate the final product. Whether
each gets a paragraph or half a paragraph, try to
allow them roughly equal time.* When developing
each, feel free to employ either doctrine or
narrative. With a concern of the text, present the
textual and exegetical material to support your
view that this is in fact a legitimate concern of the
text. If the concern of the text from the Gospel of
John text is "the wine ran out," give us enough of
the story's details to remind us of the text and

to develop the significance of this shortage. You
may find that as you write you may include some
of the other concerns of the text that you did not
select for the flow. When developing the concern
of the sermon/homily, "our good times end," play
with the words and free-associate. When have you
had an experience of good times or of good times
ending? When has someone else had this experience? If an experience comes to mind as you
daydream and you do not immediately see the
link, trust your unconscious has found a connection and work to discover what that is. Imagination often works at subconscious or intuitive
levels. In this case you might want to allow what
you say to be informed by a Christian doctrine of
time.

5. Allow the loops to be somewhat self-
contained. Trust that the positioning given to the
major concern of the text and the major concern
of the sermon/homily (*at least* at the beginning,
reversal, and ending) will create the desired
unity. Additional or frequent repetition of either
or both of these, keeping the wording the same
each time, will add further unity. *Nonetheless, the
minor concerns exist to serve the major concerns.* If
they do not, the unity will suffer. No minor
concerns are chosen simply for their own sake.
Each develops (or is shaped in the development to
serve) some aspect of relevance to the central
idea. If we have a plethora of exegetical information, much of it exciting, and if we try to do the
writing all on Saturday, we will cramp imagination and try to cram too much material into our
preaching. The congregation is not interested in
many of the intricate ideas we might find exciting

in our textual study. The reason we must spread the homiletical process and the writing over as many days as we can is to allow the material we present to come from us. Even as Garvie spoke of the need for doctrine to have the flavor of experience, so too, exegetical material should be presented to have the flavor of experience. We do not preach from the commentaries: we preach from experience. If we have allowed our material to filter through experience, it will be easier to ensure that our minor concerns serve our major one.

6. Focus on developing a *link phrase* or idea to move us into the next loop. Often this need be no more than the repetition of a key word or phrase from the last sentence written. It might be something as simple as, "The text seems to agree with this idea" or, "If we find it difficult to trust God, our experience is the same as. . . ." These links are simple but very important. They will make for a smooth flow from one loop to the next. They will also be key phrases to memorize for a smooth oral delivery. We should write for memory and overlearn (not necessarily memorize) for delivery. Memory aids for us in the sermon are hearing aids for our congregations.

7. Seek an overall balance between the story and doctrine. A biblical text that is heavily doctrinal will make more demand on our situation for story and imagery than one that is not. Similarly, a biblical text that is story will make more demand on our situation for doctrine.

8. Do not be afraid to split either a story or a discussion of a doctrine. For instance, in the law section we might in part be developing the

Christian doctrine of sin. We might talk about the manner in which the good things we try to do so often go wrong. We might then leave that discussion and come back to it somewhere in the gospel section. There we would put it in perspective of what God has done for us: God will not allow sin to have the final say. Alternatively, a story may be told in the law section and its good-news ending may be told in the gospel section. In some cases, however, we have no choice. *If we have raised an emotionally powerful law issue in the law section we must return to that issue (if not to the specific story) in the gospel section in order to suggest where good news might be found.* This splitting seems natural to the congregation and the return to the same story later in the sermon only contributes to the sense of its unity. Be careful, however: returning to the *opening* story or discussion almost always tells people that you are ending, so make sure you are.

9. The reversal, that is, the shift into the good news with the detailed development of the major concern of the text, is an arbitrary movement. There is nothing complex about it. When we are roughly halfway through our written draft (i.e., if we have fifteen minutes to preach and we have written enough for eight minutes) it is time to switch into gospel, perhaps with a simple phrase such as, "But the good news for us is. . . ." If ever you lose your way in writing, just move on to the next loop or substitute another.

10. One of the delights of this approach to writing sermons and homilies is that revisions are relatively easy. If the end product is too long, a loop can simply be removed or shortened and the link phrases recast. This kind of quick alteration is not easy in a structure where each point rests on the ones preceding it in the developing argument. Here, as long as we keep before the congregation the major concern, our preaching will have the unity we seek.

In this chapter we have been developing ways to ensure the spark between story and doctrine, the two ancient forms of faith expression. It is the spark that occurs when our experience is illuminated by doctrine or when doctrine illuminates our experience. We reflect on our experience and we seek understanding of our faith. This kind of sparking occurs at a more abstract level than our previous homiletical levels. It is nonetheless as universal a principle for preaching as the juxtaposing of biblical text and our situation or as the reconciliation of judgment and grace. And it is crucial for our preaching to reach the entire body of Christ. In our age in which commuting and television have removed much of the incentive for community-sharing in general, stories and doctrines still create communities. Stories and doctrines, like the gluten in flour, bind us to one another. God speaks to us through our stories and doctrines as they relate to the Bible, and people are hungry for them. In our next chapter we will consider the pastoral and prophetic dimensions of feeding our people.

CHAPTER FIVE

THURSDAY
FRIDAY
SATURDAY

Pastor and Prophet

The purpose of the previous chapters has been to take us one day at a time through the development of imagination for preaching. In these final days of the week, we concentrate on dwelling with our people and writing the sermon or homily in full. Dwelling with our people means in part, caring for our people. It also means naming the issues that need to be raised in our preaching. The task here is to harness the energy that springs from the juxtaposition of our roles as pastors and prophets. These are the two missions of preaching, to be nurturing people in whatever conditions they are found and to be initiating change in accordance with God's will.

Most of us experience a tension in our preaching and teaching between pastoral care and prophetic utterance. We live conscious of the gap that exists between the world as it is and God's dream for the world, recognizing that God is at work bringing the world to the promise of salvation. Even as God was willing to undergo suffering for our redemption, so too, true human power is often exercised in the non-avoidance of suffering and death. Yet social sciences have shown that we instinctively avoid pain, denying the reality it represents. The scandal of the cross, says Ronald Sunderland, "is that it forces us to decide, consciously and deliberately, whether to take it up. Only in so doing can we choose the freedom that one experiences as a slave of Christ, freedom to know and to live life to its fullest, as opposed to becoming enslaved to the passions of self-interest."[1] There is constantly this paradox of freedom through enslavement to Christ, of fullness of selfhood through denial of selfhood, that informs our mission. When we speak about a spark between the two, we are speaking about the freedom that can be ours as preachers when these two missions are reconciled. It is a spark that can illumine imaginative new avenues for ministry wherever we look.

To preachers the parish needs often seem so different from the ones on the news reports, the big items, what we often consider as the prophetic ones. To raise some of these issues seems to risk alienating some of the members or even worse, splitting the congregation. The risks seem so threatening that we find it hard to support our concern for the poor, the aged, the infirm, the abused, or future generations with a call for significant actions on their behalf. At times we feel we opt for one or the other, for unity or for action, as though they are in fact alternatives. Many of us end up raising a tough social issue one week and for the next several try to make up for it by being pastoral and gentle or loving in our focus. Few of us may yet feel confident that we know how to be both pastoral and prophetic.

For Jesus, pastor and prophet were one: we cannot separate Jesus' teachings into those about social justice and those about pastoral care. Could we say that Jesus' instruction to the rich person was more social justice than pastoral care? Could we say that the story of the Good Samaritan was more pastoral care than social justice? Both were interwoven. Both were held in tension. They were both part of his overriding concern for the weighty matters of the law—justice, mercy, and love. For us they cannot be alternatives either. Nor do they need to be, although it is the conflict between pastor and prophet that we generally perceive more frequently than the spark of their reconciliation.

Our dual roles are not a problem unless we choose to view them as such; in fact, the tension between them is creative and enabling of ministry. Daniel L. Migliore talks about the freedom that comes from a balance between the two:

> The passion of God not only motivates us to eliminate whatever suffering can be eliminated; it also empowers us to accompany our brothers and sisters into regions of darkness where suffering can no longer be eliminated; it enables

and invites us to share suffering where efforts to
overcome it prove futile; it frees us to continue a
ministry of compassion and shared grief at the
point where those who are guided by criteria of
utility and success cease their efforts.[2]

This freedom is not possible where it is thought
possible to separate pastoral and prophetic
functions. When pastor and prophet are treated
as equal and are in relationship, imagination of
the heart is set free. Our prophetic function
prevents our ministry from becoming too narrow.
Our pastoral function prevents our anger and
frustration with the sin of the world from turning
into deep-seated bitterness. Together they foster
hope and enable us to recognize God's ongoing
action in the world that brings us to the fullness of
time. Mother Teresa says there are no great acts,
just small acts done in great love. Our small
attempts to change the world are not small or
futile if they are seen as part of the action of
Christ's body around the world to bring forth
God's will. The purpose of this chapter is not so
much to create the spark that exists between
pastor and prophet as it is to prevent that spark
from being lost through undue attention to one or
the other.

Three areas of our doctrinal understanding
may need expansion if we are to juxtapose the
pastor and the prophet for preaching. Let us take
each one in turn.

1. Expanding our doctrines of time and space.
We treat our notions of time and space as though
they are absolute. Linguists tell us it is on these
two broad axes of thought that all of our language

system is built. We think of the present as cut off from the past (except for memory) and from the future (except for imagination); and yet we think of time being an irreversible one-way flow, a movement given metaphoric shape by Heraclitus early in Western thought—"You cannot step twice into the same river, for other waters and yet other waters go ever flowing on." We think of the place we live as cut off from other places by distance or by geographical or human boundaries yet we know this separateness is largely our own mental creation since we keep looking beyond the boundaries to the far horizon. Christ tells us that our notions of time and space are too limited.

Time and space are no more absolute than any number of other things we rely on to make sense of life on planet Earth. When Jesus says that all things shall pass away except his words, does he not include time and space? Is not God, alone, absolute? John Dominic Crossan was getting at this point when he said:

> The geographers tell us we do not live on firm earth but on giant moving plates whose grinding passage and tortured depths give us earthquake and volcano. Jesus tells us that we do not live in firm time but on giant shifting epochs whose transitions and changes are the eschatological advent of God. It is the view of time as [our] future that Jesus opposed in the name of time as God's present, not as eternity beyond us but as advent within us.[3]

The appropriate attitude to time and space for our teaching and preaching is given to us in our understanding of the celebration of the Lord's

Supper. We are gathered with the communion of saints, those who have gone before us, those who are alive today but in different places, and those future generations who are yet to come. Perhaps even our thinking that God's salvation history moves in a straight line needs to go as well.

C. S. Song says, "God moves in all directions: God moves forward, no doubt, but also sideways and even backwards. Perhaps God zigzags too. . . . God goes everywhere a redeeming presence is called for."[4] It is an imaginative idea that God moves back in time to redeem past suffering, and it is an exercise in imagination of the kind that marks faithful living.

We sometimes use time and space as excuses for not dealing with issues. ("It is happening somewhere else," or, "It is something our children will have to deal with.") But as Marianne H. Micks has observed, "The claim of the past on the present is . . . also the claim of the future on the present."[5] Often we do not take seriously the new time and space in which we live as Christians. Now there is no space or time that can separate us from the heartache and suffering of the world. Everyone is our neighbor. And now there is similarly no time or space that separates us from God's action in shaping human life. Now neither our words nor our actions, insofar as they embody God's Word, will or can return empty.

Thus we could argue that failure to raise justice issues in preaching is a challenge to the relevancy of the gospel. We want to claim all time and space as salvation time and space. We claim that nothing can stand in the way of God's purpose. Moreover, we claim that there is nothing that can stand in the way of our being firsthand witnesses to the resurrection today.

2. Expanding our doctrine of evil. There are three kinds of evil that theology commonly recognizes: natural evil, personal evil, and corporate or systemic (i.e., existing in human social systems) evil. It is the latter two in particular that need our attention here. When our understanding of evil, aside from natural evil, is only personal, our understanding is too limited and we will be tempted to think of our ministry as primarily pastoral. The doctrine of systemic evil affirms that even if everyone were to turn to God, there would still be evil in the world. Sin resides in social systems, not just in individuals. The most righteous people in the world could be running an institution or a business that is sinful. Jesus was addressing systemic evil when he challenged the righteous Pharisees of his day. Systemic evil is as unavoidably present in the structures of the church as in any other organization, as most of us have had occasion to observe.

Individuals participate in systems that deny justice, peace, and love. We all share a responsibility for societal sin. We share responsibility when a single mother must turn to prostitution to survive; when the cycles of child abuse or wife-battering are not broken; when hard working farm families lose their lands to the banks; or when millions face starvation in Africa. We cannot close our minds to the crucifixion of Christ today, and our role in it, and expect to understand Easter.

One of the reasons that Robert McAfee Brown wrote his *Theology in a New Key* was that he

recognized the "rude reality . . . that my joys and
fulfillments are frequently purchased at the cost
of misery and denial to others, and freedoms my
country extends to me are freedoms it denies to
small minorities at home and vast majorities
abroad."[6] Systemic evil is whatever works in our
lives to deny our connectedness to the lives and
actions of our brothers and sisters on this planet.
The best evidence of systemic evil may well be the
denial of its reality and the affirmation of only
personal sin by many well-meaning and good-
hearted Christians.

One of the implications of expanding our
understanding of evil for preaching is that our
notion of God's love will be expanded. A radical
understanding of our sin encourages a radical
understanding of God's love and grace: it is the
point Jesus made concerning the prostitute who
had had much forgiven and who therefore loved
God more than the righteous Pharisee (Luke
7:36 ff). Another implication is the recognition
that politics (by which I mean social justice issues
and partisan politics but not politicization of the
gospel, or the serving of an ideology) cannot be
avoided. The attempt to avoid politics is itself
political: it inadvertently states that things are
fine as they are. Furthermore, we recognize that
"God has acted in Jesus Christ to reclaim all
human life, including the political, social and
economic."[7]

This unavoidability of politics is one of the
reasons there is so much commotion in theology
these days. It is a recent idea that political bias
informs everything that we do and say, whether
this bias is toward rich or poor; employed or

unemployed; male or female; black, white, yellow, brown, or red. It is impossible to avoid bias. Jesus had a bias toward the underprivileged and the unwell in his ministry. We have biases too. The issue is not, How do we avoid bias but is rather, How do we become aware of our biases? and, Which biases do we choose to affirm in light of our faith? We can explore these kinds of questions with our congregations: prophetic utterance, even if it sounds like politics, need not be dismissed as irrelevant to the task of the church.

3. Expanding our doctrine of prophecy. The Old Testament tradition of true and false prophets wisely suggests that prophecy, or the gift for divine utterance, is something that cannot be taught: God calls up God's own prophets, often from people the righteous would rather not recognize. But there is nonetheless a prophetic role to which all in the church are called. Our understanding of prophecy is too limited if it is conceived as social harangue or constant social action campaigns. As Walter Brueggemann provocatively said:

> Prophetic ministry consists of offering an alternative perception of reality and in letting people see their own history in the light of God's freedom and . . . will for justice. . . . [These] are not always and need not be expressed primarily in the big issues of the day. They can be discerned wherever people try to live together and worry about their future and their identity.[8]

Stanley M. Hauerwas has a similar view, understanding hospital visitation as prophetic:

"Visiting the sick may appear to be mundane, but it is no less a prophetic task than protesting against the idolatry of the nation state. Indeed, it is, in a sense, part of the protest . . . [in] its refusal to let the state or wider society determine who it will and will not serve."[9] The prophetic ministry of the church is exercised wherever issues of justice, mercy, and love are named as issues of faith.

Our understanding of prophecy is also too limited if we think of it only as confrontational and critical. The prophetic ministry is also the dreaming ministry. Prophets provide dreams of what human society could conceivably be, re-demptive dreams that point us in new directions away from the nightmares of the past. Many poets and artists in our society function as prophets, and this is one reason the church needs to pay attention to art. Northrop Frye affirms this in arguing that totalitarian states are threatened by the arts and therefore they do not generate new art forms.[10]

Preaching is a place for art and dreaming. Brueggemann claimed several years ago that it was, "the vocation of the prophet to keep alive the ministry of imagination,"[11] and recently he has picked the idea up again in defining the prophetic task as maintaining a "destabilizing presence": "It is . . . *an assault on public imagination* aimed at showing that the present presumed world is not absolute, but that a thinkable alternative can be imagined, characterized, and lived in."[12]

But this prophetic ministry is a ministry of the congregation, not just of the preacher. The dreams we voice may be our own dreams in light of our understanding of the Scriptures, it is true, but as frequently they will be the dreams that we have gathered from listening to the members of the congregation as they seek to live out their faith (even though some may have forgotten their dreams!). It was this way for Jesus: his dreams were the great dreams of the Jewish faith about the will of God. Thus we are harvesters of our people's stories, dreamers of their dreams, interpreters of God's Word among them. We lead them and they lead us to the living out of our dreams in the land of the living.

Raising Difficult Issues

The problem of course is how to raise difficult pastoral and prophetic issues so that the lid does not blow off the pot. Two preliminary ideas need to be stressed. One is that difficult issues can be raised only if the prophetic role of the preacher is perceived to be inseparable from the pastoral role. One congregation seemed ready to dismiss their pastor at a meeting when one of the opposition said, "I don't agree with the preacher on this issue, but what I do know is that when my wife was dying he was the one who sat with me through the night." Perhaps something had gone wrong to move events so far before reconciliation. Nonetheless, if the preacher is perceived to be genuinely *with* the people, caring for them in their times of need, standing with them under the Word that is preached, the pastoral and prophetic roles are seen as wedded.

The other point is again that prophetic and pastoral issues alike arise out of the life of the congregation. When our people look in the mirror of our preaching and find their own lives reflected, they are more likely to appreciate it when the mirror reflects others. Prophetic and pastoral preaching begins in listening to and working with our people through the week. In preaching we anticipate their responses. We allow for different opinions. Since our primary task is to lead people to responsible faith decisions, we might make clear, if necessary, our own personal position on a controversial issue, but do so from the standpoint of openness and with an invitation to further discussion. There may be times, against everything we strive for, when we have to take a stand against the majority of our people and let the pieces fall where they will. Part of being an effective pastor is being able to discern whether an issue is worth this price. We may expect that we will have to pay it less often than an equinox, yet more frequently than a blue moon.

Pastoral and prophetic preaching, like the rest of worship, is nurtured by the educational and mission life of the church. There are many excellent mission and outreach resources for group study.[13] Many of our best resources, however, are the issues and people of our own communities. When there is no housing for the poor, the church can be the instrument for initiating it; when there is a strike, the church can help management and workers speak to each other; where people are crying anywhere in the world and their cries are not being heard, the church can be a megaphone. The education programs give us resources for preaching and support in carrying through the implications of preaching.

How are we to raise the difficult issues? In a moment we will turn to Jesus' own preaching for guidance, but there are some preliminary comments to be made.

David Buttrick, with his understanding that preaching alters the congregation's consciousness, outlines in a general way what must happen for a congregation's thinking to shift: there must be a description of the situation "as it presents itself to consciousness"; there must be a "rereading of the situation by Christian consciousness"; the situation must then be taken "into Christian consciousness" for reinterpretation; and, there must be portrayed a "new course of action for congregational consciousness."[14]

In addition the *manner* in which we present issues will have a bearing on how they are received. There is a poetic dimension to being a pastor and prophet. A colleague once said of William Faulkner, "Whenever you find someone writing that well about such terrible things, you know things cannot be all bad." It is a little that way about the pastor-prophet. If the preacher can raise difficult issues in a powerful and sometimes poetic way, the issues become less oppressive. Frederick Buechner has put his finger on this in speaking about "prophet-preachers":

> They put words to both the wonder and the horror of the world, and . . . because these words are poetry, are image and symbol as well as meaning, are sound and rhythm, maybe above all are passion, they set echoes going the way a

choir in a great cathedral does, only it is we who
become the cathedral and in us that the words
echo. . . . It is the experience [of truth] that they
stun us with, speaking it out in poetry which
transcends all other language in its power to open
the doors of the heart.[15]

The *form* in which we raise an issue will also
have a bearing on how it is received. If we need to
communicate some relevant facts and figures and
analysis concerning an unfamiliar issue, there is
no better way than doctrine. The facts speak for
themselves, although as Philip Wheelwright once
said, "The plain fact is that not all facts are
plain." If we need to raise *sensitive* issues and
move people to action, there is often no better way
than story. Story often functions in such a way as
to allow difficult issues to be raised and heard
without antagonism and animosity, particularly
if we use a true story of someone whose life is
profoundly affected by an issue. For one thing we
are presenting something they probably have not
heard before, a new angle on an issue that in itself
may be old and familiar. For another, the
approach is personal, about someone like you and
me, and emotional bonding is possible. And
further, the story represents an indirect appeal to
experience. We can argue with someone's *interpretation* of the facts; it is harder to argue with
someone's *experience* of them. The manner is
more invitational than confrontative.

But the obverse of this is also true, although it is
not often noted. Story can confront us more
sharply, not less, than doctrine, precisely because
it comes close to who we are. We see this in
Nathan's confrontation of King David and in the
various parables of Jesus.

Søren Kierkegaard recognized the importance of narrative in his preference for indirect communication over direct and in his thesis that God communicates with us indirectly, particularly in the revelation of Jesus Christ. Fred Craddock called this way of communicating the faith, "overhearing the gospel" in his book of that title.[16] Richard A. Jensen connects it with Emily Dickinson's, "Tell all the truth, but tell it slant."[17] And Sallie McFague finds it in the "soft focus" or "assertorial lightness" (i.e., asserting lightly) of Jesus' parables.[18] But however we describe the effect, the story is a valuable and often underutilized tool in the pastor-prophet dynamic of preaching.

One area in which most preaching using narrative has tended to be lame, with the exception of much black preaching, is the raising of social-justice concerns. One suspects at times that this is not because of the "soft focus" or "assertorial lightness" often found in the approach: rather it is because the focus is simply not present, at least in many of the published sermons, homilies, articles, and books that seem to rely on narrative. It is almost as though the power and impact of narrative may at times seduce us into comfortable silence on issues beyond personal or immediate needs. It is peculiar that the promise of story should be overlooked in this one regard. One contribution of this chapter may be to make practical suggestions for this much-neglected area.

We all inadvertently use abstract categories each day to dismiss people and their needs. For instance, words such as "poor" or "rich," "Re-

publican" or "Democrat," "emotional" or "intellectual," "sexist" or "racist" can function as
excuses for us to have little concern, much in the
same way that words such as "Samaritan,"
"sinner," and "Gentile" functioned in Jesus' day.
Even the mention today of the word "abortion"
has people ready to either accept or dismiss
outright what is said. With such words as this we
do not often find ourselves saying, "Oh, I would
like to hear what those against my position say
about that." The word in itself does not invite
open listening to hear something new. Like many
other trigger-words, it can shut down imagination. Sometimes things need to be named for
what they are. But if we are trying to persuade,
the wrong word used as part of an argument
might alienate the very people who most need to
hear what we are saying. If we do what Jesus did
in using parables and tell a story, people are
sometimes involved before they realize a claim is
being made on them.

Jesus' frequent way of raising difficult issues
was to tell stories. Our frequent way can be that
too. Here by stories we mean stories based in real
life that bring the events of the world before the
Word with gratifying and sometimes painful
clarity. Our educational systems generally have
not prepared us well either to be creative or to
value story for this kind of mission purpose. The
German theologian Johann Metz is one of the
people boldly calling for story. History and
theology has been rigidified, he says, into "reflection that cannot be affected by collective historical fears or threats. . . . The present state of
meaning has had all its wrinkles ironed out and is

free of all contradictions. It is, as it were, 'hope-
lessly total.' "[19] What he, Robert Schreiter,[20] and
others are advocating is a new approach to
history, a rewriting of history that would not lose
individual stories in the attempt to distill
meaning and overall direction. Christian ethicists
also are claiming the essential role of story in a
method for ethical action: Roger Hutchinson and
Gibson Winter claim that the first step must be to
identify the community stories that stand as
paradigms, ones which "illumine and empower
the people's struggle."[21] Stanley Hauerwas similarly views story as an essential way "to locate
ourselves in relation to others, our society, and
the universe": it is through identifying those
individual stories that we then relate to the true
story of God's struggle and promise to reclaim the
world.[22] A variety of disciplines have just recently
begun to pay more attention to stories of the poor,
women, blacks, illegal immigrants, and other
oppressed or struggling groups.

It is also important for us to recognize the
importance of story in releasing the spark
between pastor and prophet. Story is the primary
firsthand record of suffering and injustice. It is by
story that people recount their own experiences of
suffering. *In preaching there is an order of priority
for story and doctrine on social-justice issues: first
we need to hear the firsthand stories of those
actually involved; second we need to hear their
reflections on their experience; and then and only
then can we benefit from reflections from outside the
context (our own included).* Unfortunately for
preaching, most of the denominational material

we receive from our various missions (from inner-city to foreign) provide us with reflections and analysis without the firsthand stories we need for continued mission emphasis in preaching. But perhaps in our own parish contexts we also tend to overlook the firsthand recounting of events. We can understand our own gathering of community stories as part of a larger movement for local communities to take seriously their own stories as one way of doing theology.

What are the community's stories and issues? They are obviously not the stories we have in confidence (even if they are from a former parish) and the congregation should have no doubt about this. Nor are they long accounts of the horror stories the congregation knows too well from this week's newspaper and television, stories that may require only the briefest mention to bring them before us. In this regard the pastor-prophet is not unlike the journalist who is ever watching for an important story, or a fresh angle on an old and familiar one. It might be the story of a man in prison or a woman with no income. It might be a story of teenagers taken from a newspaper or magazine that most of our people would not have read. The story could be of sorrow or of joy, something we have discovered in art or seen in the daily world. It is these stories that bear close resemblance to our experience of the world and that serve to break down the barriers between us and our neighbors. *Whatever stories we raise we want to remember that preaching should never become overwhelmed with the weight of the world.* Quite the opposite is true. It is there that the world is put into the perspective of faith that celebrates the good news that God's redemptive promise embraces this world.

Let us turn now to consider briefly how Jesus dealt with pastoral and prophetic issues in his preaching.

Learning from Jesus' Preaching

We learn from the manner in which Jesus dealt with pastoral and prophetic issues in his own ministry: where he chose to tread, when he kicked the dust from his sandals, with whom he chose to dine and to wash his feet, whose feet he chose to wash. We assume that all of Jesus' recorded words were addressing the needs for knowledge and for salvation, but we want to go beyond these to some of the issues implied in his teachings. Here we will briefly consider not only some of his parables *per se*, but also some of his other stories as having parabolic significance.

Normally, we think of the parables of Jesus as religious stories. They make explicitly religious points. If we consider the parables from the standpoint of imagination, something that has been largely ignored in the past, we see that they are not religious stories. They have two parts, what we will call the *story* and the religious *idea* alongside which the story is brought. Between these there is a spark that is the meaning of the parable for its context.

A different kind of two-part structure in the parable has been identified by biblical scholars. For instance, Dan Otto Via speaks of the "in meaning" and "through meaning" of parables[23] and Eta Linnemann distinguishes between the "picture part," that is the narrative, and the "reality part," that is where the parable intersects at one point of correspondence with the reality of the listener and the speaker.[24] But these discussions have been geared to help us *understand* the parables. They have stopped short of helping us *create* parables or understand how Jesus *created* them. As art students know, one of the best ways to appreciate and understand art is to try to create it, occasionally imitating the great artists. Similarly, one of the best ways of knowing how to preach the parables is to know how Jesus created them. In other words biblical studies have stopped short of exploring imagination. Thus Linnemann's "reality part" directs us to the meaning of the parable and the "picture part" serves as the vehicle toward that goal.

But rather like our approach to travel on this continent, it is frequently the destination that is more important to enjoy than is the getting to the destination. As preachers we tend to rush to the meaning and often do not tarry long studying the story itself, as though it had no value in itself. To skip the story in this way means we also skip how Jesus did it, how he was so effective in his preaching. For preaching we need the "exegete to understand" approach of biblical scholars, but we also need the "create to understand" approach we can gain from our knowledge of imagination. Jesus was a poetic genius, but in creating his parables and stories he used basic techniques that we can use to strengthen our own preaching on tough issues.

The reason the parables are so effective is that they embody imagination. As we have said, the

polarity of a parable is created by a story brought
adjacent to an idea. The juxtaposition of the two
creates a spark that gives us the meaning of the
parable. While the precise "idea" may vary, there
is one general idea that Jesus brings alongside his
stories to make them into parables. It is the idea of
the Realm (Kingdom) of God: this Realm is in
contrast to the ways of the conventional world.
Some people have difficulty with the concept of
the Realm of God, unsure of how it differs from
traditional understandings of heaven or else
unclear as to how it relates to human interaction.
It may be thought of as any location or event in
which God's justice, mercy, and love are breaking
in.

Another way of thinking about it is given by
James Breech. If he is correct in his assessment of
Jesus' teachings, the idea focuses on what it
means to be human, rooted in the power of God:
"It is to be contrasted with, on the one hand,
existing as a member of a group, and on the other
with existing as a solitary individual.[25] In the
parables this idea is sometimes stated explicitly
("the Realm of God is like . . .") and sometimes it
is implied through connecting the story with one
of the ideas we normally associate with God's
rule: love, peace, mercy, justice, righteousness,
forgiveness, discipleship, prayer, or whatever.
Less frequently, the inverse of the Realm of God is
the idea: the punishment awaiting the unprepared. But whatever the variation, *it is the linking
of this one idea, the Realm of God, to a simple story
that makes a parable.*

The reason we tend to think of the parables as
religious stories is that we rush to their overall

meaning, losing sight of the basic polarity between story and adjacent idea. The parables as a whole are religious—the stories Jesus uses in the parables are not.[26] As we will see in a moment, this perception can be freeing for us.

Most of Jesus' other stories (i.e., those that are not parables *per se*) are also not religious. They often have *parabolic significance* since they are juxtaposed with a context in Jesus' ministry, and it is out of the tension between the context and story that the meaning of these stories arise. Like the stories in the parables, they are generally about ordinary, mundane reality. Where they are not, they are at any rate about the kinds of events that commonly occur in any society: disasters, political skulduggery, murder, fraud, as well as acts of great kindness and generosity. Of course he often took the common and exaggerated it, sometimes subtly and gradually, for effect, as in the story of a mustard seed growing not just into a tall plant, as it does in the Middle East, but into a bush for birds to nest (Matt. 13:31-33). But this does not alter that Jesus was a poet who, like most poets, had trained himself to see the common things, events, and people that most of us dismiss before they register in our conscious thought. Moreover, Jesus knew how to take the ordinary and make it extraordinary by allowing language to work in powerful ways.

It has often been noted how common is the material Jesus uses for his stories. But it is one thing to note the commonness and it is another to note it *with the intention of seeing similar stories around us:* when wheat and tares grow up together, the farmer decides to wait until harvest

(Matt. 13:24 ff.). In sowing, some seed falls on the path, among rocks, among thorns, and on good soil (Luke 8:5 ff.). New wine splits old wineskins (Luke 5:37 ff.). A fig tree sprouts its leaves at an exact time (Luke 21:29 ff.). A lamp is lit in order to give light (Matt. 5:14). Vultures gather around a dead body (Luke 17:37). A parent throws a child's bread to the dogs (Matt. 15:26). A shepherd loses a sheep from the flock and goes to find it (Matt. 18:12-13). Some people who had been fishing sort their catch into good and bad (Matt. 13:47 ff.). A righteous person prayed proudly while a sinner prayed humbly (Luke 18:10 ff.). A friend needs to borrow food for a late-night visitor (Luke 11:5 ff.). One son agreed to work and did not while another refused to work but changed his mind (Matt. 21:28-29). Some bridesmaids were ready for the wedding and some were not (Matt. 25:1 ff.). Two people try to sort out their differences out of court (Matt. 5:25 ff.). Jesus' stories could not be more ordinary. They record ordinary events he saw around him as he traveled. They are of the sort that we see around us everywhere.

Some, however, were events that were more newsworthy, although still common to many communities. People would have recognized some of the stories he told as events that had recently happened and were being talked about in the public places. We may not have paused to recognize this. If they had had tabloid newspapers, we could imagine some of the headlines: tenants kill landlord's son (Luke 20:9 ff.); Siloam tower falls killing eighteen (Luke 13:5); local man appointed distant governor by Rome—servants betray while gone (Luke 19:11 ff.); local resident

buys ancient treasure in buying field (Matt.
13:44); rich person dies planning life of ease (Luke
12:16 ff.); ruler opens wedding banquet to public—ejects those not properly dressed (Matt.
22:1 ff.); persistent woman wins judgment from
harsh judge (Luke 18:2-5); labor dispute erupts
over equal pay (Matt. 20:1 ff.); government troops
massacre Galileans at worship service (Luke
13:1-3); visitor rescues mugging victim (Luke
10:30 ff.); and we could identify more. They are
stories of the widest range of events possible.
Many were about specific people.[27] If some of
Jesus' stories were not actual events, they
certainly could have been. We never hear the
disciples asking the kinds of questions we ask of
stories: "Yes, but was it true? Did it really
happen?" Jesus' stories were so common there
was no need to ask this. Instead they asked, "Yes,
but what does it mean?" They were not asking
this about the stories themselves; they were
self-explanatory. It was the ideas Jesus was
connecting with the stories that caused the
problem.

For our preaching there is no difficulty in
finding stories every place we go similar to the
kind that Jesus told, stories from flat tires to
lotteries, from neighbors putting up a fence to
international politics, and from gardening to
family squabbles. In the previous chapter we
dealt with finding stories around us and while it is
helpful to recognize that Jesus did this, that is not
our focus here. Here we want to discover how
Jesus dealt with difficult issues in his preaching
and teaching to see what we might learn for our
own preaching. To do this, obviously, we must at

least assume the plausible contexts in which he used his stories, even though many are lost to us.

There are three ways in which Jesus dealt with difficult issues of pastoral and prophetic significance in his speech. The first way made *direct use of doctrine.* The instances of this are both numerous and obvious: the Beatitudes, indeed much of the Sermon on the Mount, including the instructions on divorce and adultery, as well as the seven woes in Matthew 23, are ready instances of direct and forceful instruction and proclamation. The direct route using doctrine may be the one we most frequently tend to use in our preaching, particularly in dealing with large societal issues such as poverty or peace, and is the route that tends to dominate preaching.

Jesus also made *direct use of story.* Thus on the theme of riches he not only proclaims that the poor are blessed, that it is hard for the rich to enter the Realm of God, and that one should lend to those from whom no repayment is expected but he also tells stories directly hitting at the rich: treasure on earth is attacked by moths and rust (Matt. 6:19 ff.); the rich fool; the rich person and Lazarus. On the subject of prayer he not only tells the disciples directly how to pray (pray in secret and the Lord's Prayer) but he tells elsewhere the story of the Pharisee and the publican. On the subject of love he says love one another but he also tells the story of the Good Samaritan. In these stories there is a clear connection between the story and the subject at hand: no confusion is possible about what he meant. It is the sort of approach that we frequently use when we do employ story in our preaching. For example, in trying to address discreetly the lack of welcome shown to visitors to the congregation, we might tell a story of our visiting another church on holidays and knowing how it feels to be ignored.

Jesus' third approach to difficult issues made *indirect use of story*. This is probably the most intriguing to us, partly because it demands the most of the listener, and it is the hardest to understand how Jesus achieved the effect that he did. For our preaching on difficult issues it will be helpful if we distinguish between two kinds of indirect issue-related preaching that Jesus used: one functions at a *conscious* level and the other at a *subliminal* level.

The former, indirect use of story to affect the listener at a *conscious* level, occurs whenever Jesus is dealing with a particular issue and he tells a story that at first may seem to have no connection to the issue at hand. The listeners know that there is some connection to be made (some meaning to be found), and they consciously strive to discover what it is. Mark has a theological reason for the disciples not under-standing what Jesus says, a motif that we often refer to as Mark's messianic secret (until the resurrection it was impossible for the disciples to understand who Jesus was and what he meant), but their numerous times of bafflement at his words generally are because of indirect instruc-tion with a story that is meant to engage the listener. Most of the parables proper fall in this category: those that deal with the general "Realm of God is like . . . " (a mustard seed, a woman looking for a lost coin) and not a specific issue concerning the Realm (like the nature of discipleship or prayer) as well as those parables that give us no specific clue as to why they were originally told (the Prodigal Son). With all stories in the indirect mode, we know something is being implied about the Realm of God but no more precise issue in the original context generally penetrates the text.

Our teaching and preaching can benefit from more frequent use of indirect story to affect our listeners at a conscious level. This is the most difficult aspect of Jesus' preaching for us to imitate, the creating of our own parables, but it can be done. Jesus might frequently have started with a good story and then connected it to the intended idea. "The Realm of God is like this," he might have said to himself in order to see if it were true—to see if in fact there was a legitimate point of correspondence. But since we are talking about preaching on difficult issues, let us take that as our starting point.

There are four simple steps to follow in creating a parable: (1) state the issue (it will be the idea alongside which we will bring a story); (2) identify the human struggle behind the issue; (3) tell a story (long or short) about a different issue but involving the same struggle, making sure to say what happened (something good or bad needs to occur); and (4) preface the story with a phrase that establishes the issue, idea, or point of comparison. We often think of the parables as having a particular "twist" within them: this twist is produced by this juxtaposition of story and idea.

Let us try to write a couple of parables together.

PARABLE ONE

ISSUE: World hunger. HUMAN STRUGGLE: Looking for food and not finding it. STORY: We want a story about people looking for something and not finding it. The story must not be one about hunger, however. As I write this I hear a distant game of tennis being played and the players often go looking for the stray balls. If we add the PREFACE we get: World hunger is like (preface) the couple who had to stop playing tennis because some children in the bush ran off with their stray tennis balls (story).

PARABLE TWO

ISSUE: Teenage drug use. HUMAN STRUGGLE: The search for fulfillment in the wrong way. STORY: We want a story of someone who is not using drugs but is also seeking fulfillment in the wrong way with devastating results. Work tends to be my own "drug." Adding the PREFACE we get: Teenage drug use is like (preface) the woman who took on two jobs so that she could support her family better and in the process saw her marriage break and her family dissolve (story).

PARABLE THREE AND FOUR

These two parables were based on incidents that I saw, and the reader may be able to discern how they were created. In the first the issue is forgiveness and in the second it is poverty.

Three Being forgiving is like the police officer who gave a parking ticket and took it off when he recognized the unmarked car as his own.

Four Justice (or the inbreaking of God's Realm) is like the rich owners of the deli arriving on opening day to discover the bag-lady sleeping in the doorway.

In creating parables we are not out just to tell stories of the Realm of God but to alert ourselves and our people to the Realm of God breaking in everywhere. We clearly are not looking for one-to-one correspondence, with each detail of the story fitting some idea we are trying to represent. That is allegory, not parable. The story of the police officer would be treated as allegory if we thought that God was the officer, we were the car, and the ticket was God's forgiveness.

Obviously parables demand so much of the listeners we could not use them very often in our preaching, or if we did we might feel compelled to use the kind of commentary that Mark so often provides. We would also not use parables as a substitute for more direct handling of the issues, either with story or doctrine. This is not to discount the possible effectiveness of our own parables in raising tough issues relevant to the faith. Our parables can be particularly useful if we do not harp on the same issue week after week, like a disc jockey with one record. An issue may have been dealt with more directly in previous sermons or homilies and can be raised in parable form simply to raise that familiar issue quickly and with power.

In addition we may remember that *the act of preaching on particular biblical texts is in itself a parabolic process.* We do not have to be creating parables *per se* in order to use Jesus' approach. When we take a story from a text and hold it adjacent to a contemporary situation or issue (a concern of the text adjacent to a concern of the sermon/homily), we have already created a parabolic structure composed of story, idea, and spark, as we saw in depth in chapter 2. Whenever the issue we choose to bring alongside the text is not identical to the issue in the text itself, we have chosen the route of indirect yet conscious appeal.

There is one aspect of Jesus' dealing with issues that we have yet to develop. We said that he used two kinds of indirect preaching using story, one *conscious* and the other *subliminal.* Subliminal communication operates below the threshold of conscious thought. While it produces no sensation it is strong enough to influence mental processes and behavior. We have all been affected by subliminal messages in advertising. For instance when cigarettes are advertised by young healthy happy people the subliminal message communicated is that smoking is good for you and will make you a success. Television advertising has been banned in some places from flashing such messages as "Buy Apple Toothpaste" on the screen so briefly that the message does not register consciously, for marketing surveys have shown the effectiveness of this approach in affecting our behavior. To some degree we already pay attention to subliminal messages in preaching—we check to see how this or that will be received by Hank Simms or Marjorie Brown. We want to be learning to use subliminal communication effectively.

Jesus gives many subliminal issues (and messages about those issues) in his preaching. Whether he was aware of these need not concern us here. We do not need to make Jesus into a humorless workaholic whose words at every level convey theological intent. But the fact is that with some stories, issue-related messages are there. They are not the immediate issues with which Jesus is dealing. For instance, in the parable of the lost coin there is a subliminal issue of the need for persistence and a subliminal message that patience has a reward. Do we not think of the woman at some level as a model of how to behave if something is lost, even though we know this is not the purpose of the parable? In the prodigal son there is the subliminal issue of paternal love, and the subliminal message that this father (although neglecting his responsibilities as a father in his initial act) models how to love. There are other subliminal messages as well, such as that the elder son was right to work and the younger son was right to return home to the Jewish community. In the parable of the friend at midnight, there is a subliminal issue of hospitality and a subliminal message that we are to care for the needs of our guests. The parable of the unjust steward is interesting because it is, by our standards, an immoral story about a man who cheats his boss and continues to cheat him in settling accounts. Yet if we look at the subliminal messages we find that while the steward is praised for his ingenuity, there is no encouragement for us to cheat our bosses. The subliminal issue is business etiquette and the subliminal message is that he is dishonest and dishonesty earns dismissal.

It is possible that in telling the parable of the unjust judge, Jesus was raising on a subliminal level an issue that might have dangerous political overtones: the legal system tolerates corruption. If we are to accept Kenneth E. Bailey's interpretation of "Foxes have holes, birds of the air have nests, but the Son of man has nowhere to lay his head," Jesus was dealing with the subliminal issue of Roman occupation and the subliminal message was an illegal protest that Israel was oppressed.[28]

We need to be cautious in dealing with subliminal issues in Jesus' preaching: subliminal also means peripheral—they miss the heart of the text and are probably not what we would choose to preach on. They are the messages that seep through the text, like water through weeping tiles, almost in spite of it. James Breech and others argue, for instance, that "parables do not function in order to provide . . . models."[29] Nonetheless, in the prodigal son we absorb the father's behavior as a kind of model at some precritical, preconscious, or subliminal level, in the same way that most of us inadvertently (and sometimes otherwise) create role models from those who have influenced our lives. We cannot discern issue-related subliminal messages in all of Jesus' stories. Similarly, we cannot dismiss their impact when they are present, and when they resonate with some aspect of the faith we try to live.

One import for preaching is this: when preaching on an issue using a story, we can deal with another issue at the same time on a subliminal level. Thus in dealing with teenage drug abuse, above, we also dealt with the danger of undue devotion to work. Thus in dealing with forgiveness there was an opportunity to portray the police in a human way. Fred B. Craddock notes that if a child is afraid of a dog we do not just tell the child not to be afraid. Instead we "re-image" the idea of dog by buying a puppy. Similarly, he says, if in preaching we "re-image" through stories some groups that receive prejudice, so they are seen in a new light (as Jesus did with the good Samaritan), over time we will alter the old images and replace them with new ones.[30] This is a good instance of what can be subliminal handling of issues.

Another import for preaching is that *to preach on a major issue at any time requires that a language of common assent be established.* Over the course of time the preaching should have established the expectation that issues of importance will be raised, not always directly or in doctrinal fashion. The familiarity of these recurrent relevant concerns helps establish a shared language base between preacher and congregation out of which faith discussions may sprout. If on the other hand the preacher does not regularly touch on issues (even if only subliminally), and if the congregation has not grown accustomed to these stories seeding the sermon or homily in a variety of ways, then on the Sunday in which an issue of substance is raised, the congregation is likely to be unprepared or unwilling to hear.

What have we learned from Jesus' use of story to help us deal with pastoral and prophetic issues in our preaching? We have learned several things, one being that we too can raise issues by using stories of everyday events around us. We have seen that in addition to dealing with issues in a direct doctrinal way, we have several alternatives with story: *we may use a story that deals directly with an issue; we may use a story that deals indirectly with an issue but demands that the hearer make conscious the connection; and we may use story indirectly to communicate on an issue at a subliminal level.*

Guidelines for Raising Issues

But there is more to a gift than the gift itself: there is the wrapping and the way it is given. Similarly there is more to using story to deal with an issue than the story form: there is the style in which it is told. Here too, we may learn from Jesus. We observed earlier that biblical scholars, because of their focus on the goal of meaning, have been silent about creativity. In part this has meant for homiletics that while we were aware of the commonness of the subject matter Jesus used, we may have rushed to the meaning of the parables and not taken the further small but important step of imitating Jesus' method— looking to the common *around us* to create our own stories. In his *History of the Synoptic Tradition,* Rudolph Bultmann examined the storytelling techniques of Jesus and his contemporaries.[31] Theirs was an oral culture. Once again most of us in homiletics have taken Bultmann's stylistic laws and seen them primarily as being descriptive of the parables instead of being prescriptive for us in our storytelling. From what better culture is there for preachers to learn about using story than from Jesus' oral one?

I will list some of the more important rules Bultmann discovered, adding my own comments and also giving a few additional guidelines to keep in mind for using story to deal with issues:

1. Be concise. Only the necessary persons appear. There is a similar economy governing the description of events or actions. Anything unnecessary is omitted (Bultmann). To this encouragement to be compact and concise we might add: less is more but too little is not enough. This general rubric applies to all of our preaching but it certainly applies to stories. When the preacher tells the entire plot of a movie or novel, generally we no longer want to see it. We do well to read good book and movie reviews to study how critics give only enough detail to tantalize. When using contemporary art, it is a good rule to pick out only one image or event or issue from a book or movie and let that stand as a symbol of the whole. For instance, if we saw the 1984 movie *Country* we might tell the scene in which the teenage boy is at the auction of his grandfather's midwest farm, the mortgage of which is being foreclosed. When the old and treasured harness comes on the auction block, the grandfather looks on in stony silence. And then, when the highest bid is only two dollars, the grandson bids $28.65 and gives the harness to the old man. In telling stories and in preaching as a whole, we should be leaving our people comfortably fed, perhaps hungering for more, but never so filled they do not want to move.

2. The law of stage duality says that only two people acting or speaking are present at one time. There are never more than three characters.

Groups are treated as a single person (Bultmann). This simple guideline, if observed, can mean the difference between a story being understood and it going over the heads of some.

3. Stories are told from a single perspective (Bultmann). Thus in the prodigal son the camera follows the prodigal. Events are told in sequence with no simultaneous coverage and no flashbacks to the home scene while the prodigal is away. If we are considering how to relate a complex series of events, this law can be helpful if we allow it to instruct our writing and editing. This law can have contrasting implications in another direction for preaching. Some preachers try to preach from a single perspective by turning the entire sermon or homily into literally one story, perhaps retelling the biblical story in ancient or contemporary idiom. It sounds simple but it is the most difficult of all preaching formats to bring off well: if it fails it generally fails badly with both doctrine and story suffering. The risk may not be worth it.[32]

4. Portray characters by their actions or a particular attribute, like the judge who "feared not God or regarded people." For the most part people are characterized by what they say or do, or how they behave. Let the actions speak for themselves and leave out motives, feelings, and descriptions not essential to the action (Bultmann). In other words, create it, do not relate it. In my experience of getting a novel published, the hardest thing to do is to leave out of a story any commentary or interpretation, any of my own feelings, and any naming of the feelings of the characters. All of these should emerge through the speech and unraveling of events. We should see that someone is angry. We should not be told.

5. No conclusion is necessary if it is self-evident or irrelevant (Bultmann). Avoid nailing down the story too tightly. The sermon or homily should not be the story's coffin. Instead, trust the meaning of the story to be apparent by the context in which it is placed. The process is called favoring understatement to overstatement. If we are uncomfortable with the ambiguity of life we may be uncomfortable with the ambiguity of story. To make stories fit too tightly into their interpretive framework is to rob them of some of their meaning. If you feel you overtell your stories, try writing them out and then cut off the first and last sentences: then you may have your story.

The same possible lack of need for a conclusion may be true for the sermon or homily as a whole. There is rarely a need to "tie everything up" with a neat doctrinal summary of everything that has been said. A simple reminder of the road we have been traveling (in the form of an explicit return to the major concern of the text and/or the major concern of the sermon/homily, possibly in the context of a good news story) is generally sufficient. This format is invitational, inviting the people to live out the Good News, and is somewhat open-ended. It recognizes that at least from a faith perspective, a sermon or homily is not completed in the church on Sunday; it ends in the life and work of the people throughout the week.

6. Direct speech and soliloquy are used where possible (Bultmann). Do not say what someone said, let us hear the actual speech. This can be particularly useful if, instead of saying, "God sometimes seems far away," we turn it into, for instance, a question placed on the lips of the congregation: "Do we not cry out in the night saying, 'Where are you God? Why do you leave me so alone?'" Direct speech attributed by us to someone in a biblical story can also be a way of conveying some important pieces of exegetical material.

7. The law of repetition suggests threefold repetition. The law of end-stress suggests the most important thing is left to the end (Bultmann). We see this for instance in the Good Samaritan, where three people pass by, or in the great supper, where three guests make their excuses. We need not fear formalizing the structure of our stories (i.e., "and a second time she came to him"). We have already adopted this in principle for the sermon or homily as a whole in recommending that the major concern of the text and/or the major concern of the sermon/homily be located at minimum at the beginning, middle, and ending.

Turning now to some of my own:

8. Pick stories that are different from the text's story. Any text can speak to any situation. If the biblical text is dealing with power and authority in the synagogue or early church, do not be confined to those issues in our world. Go outside the church to where power and authority are big issues for the congregation, perhaps in the workplace, or at school, or in the home. The greater the distance between the text's story and our own, the more powerful may be the "spark" we create.

9. Pick difficult issues and stories that put pressure on the text. We can be like Jacob, except that we are demanding a blessing from the particular biblical text. It is in confronting the tough pastoral and prophetic issues that the text really comes alive and the radical impact of God's Word is experienced. Do not stay with the story of the woman who prayed and her husband got better; go also to the story of the woman who prayed and her husband did not get better. Do not stay with the story of the good teenager; go to the one who got in trouble and struggle with what the Good News might be for him. In suggesting the Good News for these tough situations we are right to be somewhat tentative with such phrases as, "Could it be . . . ?" or "Is it possible that . . . ?" rather than to risk being presumptuous. We are Brueggemann's prophet dreaming alternate realities. We should always test what we are doing by saying, "So what? What difference does it make?" and we should make sure the difference is apparent.

10. Select stories from a wide variety of life experiences. Some students make the mistake of transposing concerns of the text into specifically religious contexts every time. Thus "the disciples follow Jesus" becomes "we follow Jesus" and, with other similar transpositions, the stories all end up focusing on the church. The result can be claustrophobic. Transpositions that are not specifically religious offer interesting material to imagination. If the above is transposed it becomes, "the world looks for someone to follow" or, "we are not sure who we follow." In a different vein, one student of mine realized that all of his stories had to do with male athletes. There were two problems here: not everyone relates to sports and not everyone is male. Many of us men fail to make sure that at least half of our stories are about and from women. We may all need to make sure that we give a balanced picture of both sexes in the stories we relate—change the sex if necessary in the retelling of the story. Many of us in the middle class fail to tell stories that give the perspective of the poor. If quoting a source that uses sexist language, we can change that language in the sermon or homily the same way we would change it in a written report, with square brackets or footnotes that are not part of the oral delivery. (Afterward we can explain what we have done, if someone asks.) Further to ensure that the range of our stories is sufficiently broad and inclusive, we might learn from the Roman Catholic guide to the prayers for mass. It suggests *four categories that we could use for preaching: personal, local (the community at large), church (the church universal), and world*. In using these, a personal story about an international personality like Princess Diana is still a personal story since it does not raise a world issue.

11. Use personal stories (although caution flags should be present if we use more than one or two about ourselves each time we preach). The old rubric of avoiding personal reference was well founded—the pulpit is not the place for a spotlight on the preacher but on God's Word. The avoidance backfired, however, with the preacher often being perceived as above God's Word. *There*

*is a difference between a personal story and a private
story, and the latter should never be used.* When
personal stories are used, they are never to put the
preacher in an angelic light ("when I was making
my sixteenth visit this week . . . "). Rather they are
used when telling a story of someone else might be
unfair or when for pastoral reasons it is important
that the congregation have glimpses that the
pastor struggles too. It is the preacher's vulnerability that the congregation needs occasionally to
experience, not recitals of the preacher's virtue or
lack of virtue. Stories that show our vulnerability
(our doubts, mistakes, and humanity) are to be
distinguished from stories that evoke our own
emotional fragility or tears as we tell them. If we
have not yet resolved in some fashion the emotional issues behind a story, it may be too soon to
tell it. At the same time, passion is necessary for
preaching. The primary use of personal stories is to
evoke from the congregation their own experiences, not to place the preacher front and center in
a manner that will detract from the Word.
Furthermore, personal stories need not be only
about the preacher. In dealing with tough issues,
tell personal stories about the people involved in
the issues. We thereby resist some of the dehu-
manizing tendency of the world.

12. Prefer stories of ordinary people in
non-trivial situations. Stories of people like
Mother Teresa should be used with great caution
(unless we have a firsthand item to share, perhaps
a story about the time we saw her in person). They
have a predictable quality about them. The
occasional story of a great person may inspire us,
but frequent use of these stories affects us as law:

the congregation can only seem inadequate by comparison. Moreover, these stories suggest that manifestations of Christ's action in the world cannot be found nearer to home.

13. Stay with stories that are or sound real. In a large congregation, fifteen minutes of sermon or homily time may represent one or two hundred listening hours of which we are the stewards. Avoid allegories, in which every detail of the story corresponds to some moral point; they rarely work and almost always twist reality out of recognizable shape. Avoid appealing to the beauty of nature as evidence of God; nature can disclose mystery, but it is the revelation of Jesus Christ, not nature, that is the truth to which we appeal. Generally avoid fairy stories or stories about knights in armor that, apart from their sex-role stereotyping, are difficult to tell in a convincing way or to make explicitly Christian. And avoid cute stories about little boys and girls whose names are always Jimmy and Sally. Give real people who live in some real place, who eat real foods with particular brand names, and whose stories are not happily ever after with all mystery and ambiguity gone. Leave the ambiguity in the story. Specific details make a story more accessible than general descriptions. Although in telling some stories we may need to alter some details for pastoral or other reasons, we should still be able to say yes when asked afterward, "Was that story true?" (provided that it was not told tongue-in-cheek!). The person who asks may really be asking, "May I trust the truth I came to see while you were preaching?"

14. Find ways to name your own feelings (not

just your thoughts) about the issues you raise and about your raising them now. This will assist the congregation in hearing what you are saying. We are employing imagination of the heart and everything we say should connect to the hearts of our people.

15. Give issues in our situation the same kind of careful background exegesis as was given to the biblical text. Avoid generalizations. Get the facts straight.

16. Finally, and somewhat lightly, there is the importance of not being earnest. So much has been said on the other side of this issue that it is time a word was said against the identification of the pulpit and the furrowed brow. It is a word for humor, even in raising serious issues. In fact, humor by its nature is always about serious issues, issues that matter.[33] Many of the biblical texts contain humor, or elements that may strike us as humorous. We hold the texts in reverence, which means that we never mock the texts, but it also means honoring the laughter they may contain. This is not to encourage those who at times turn the pulpit into a podium for the stand-up comic. Jokes should be used with greatest caution and only when they are worked into the fabric of what is being said. The best humor is the preacher's own natural humor that comes out of the preacher daring to be a real person before the congregation.

Methodology

How do the pastoral and prophetic issues we raise from our contemporary situations connect with the concerns of the sermon/homily? By definition these concerns deal with our situation and hence already represent our issues. If there are some issues with which you know you must deal (one pastor calls these issues "prayer concerns"),[34] keep them nearby as you plan the flow and incorporate them into the transposing of the concerns of the text into the concerns of the sermon/homily.

The central idea (i.e., the major concern of the text and the major concern of the sermon/homily) can help us name the congregation's issue that underlies it. We should try to phrase this in their own words within the sermon or homily itself. For instance, if preaching on Luke 9:51-62, at the beginning of Luke's long travel section, we might take our major concern of the text to be: "Jesus sets his face toward Jerusalem." Since Jerusalem means crucifixion and our salvation, our major concern of the sermon/homily might be: "Jesus sets his face toward our freedom." The theme here is freedom and the issue might be: we long to be free (i.e., of work, of relationships, of financial or health worries). Naming this in the preaching might be done by framing it in our words, placing it on our lips, and using direct (perhaps first person) speech. This becomes the primary need that you will address, the primary pastoral and prophetic issue with which you will deal.

The process is essentially the same if we are preaching at a special occasion, such as a baptism, anniversary, or wedding. Behind each of these occasions there is a congregational issue, an issue provided by the occasion. Any text can speak to any situation, we simply need to identify what the issue is that needs to be addressed. For instance, at baptism the theme might be membership in the church and the issue might be: we all need to know that we belong. In the preaching we might present it this way: "In everything that child did she seemed to be saying, just like us, 'I only want to belong. I just want to know that I matter. I need to know that someone cares.'" Our major concerns would address this issue and this issue would shape their development.

We have been saying that the primary function of preaching is an invitation to faith. But faith is not faith unless it is lived. In other words, *we are inviting people to faith and to live out that faith in action.* It is because we have experienced the freedom of Christ that we seek to bring freedom to God's people, whatever their circumstances might be and whatever form of Christian ministry that might involve. There are throughout the sermon or homily, and perhaps particularly toward the end, opportunities to *suggest a specific action (or actions) that might embody the truth we have heard proclaimed.* What we have said about law, however, still applies. We do not now resort to the "musts" and "shoulds" we have been working to overturn in the gospel section. Even the action to which we might point is presented in an invitational manner. It might sound like this: "In our baptism we accepted the freedom that Christ will not permit us to let go. What a wonderful freedom that is. The barriers that keep us from loving or that prevent us from daring to visit in the prison—they can bind us no longer. They are already overcome in Christ. Freedom is ours. It is in acting that we will discover that freedom."

Ideally we may start to write on Wednesday, and do the bulk of the writing on Thursday, or perhaps Friday at the latest. For imagination of the heart we need several days, with some work each day, in order to be able to present complex ideas in a simple, clear, and fresh fashion by the end of the week. What we say must come from us and be filtered through experience. It is often a good idea to take a break between writing the law and gospel sections. The reason is simple. When we write about people in specific law situations we begin, like good actors, acting in roles, to experience their suffering. A brief time away from the sermon/homily writing will allow us to distance some of those important feelings and to make a fresh start on the gospel. Sometime on Saturday come back to the finished manuscript; in the meantime small, polishing ideas and link phrases will have come to mind. If you are going to do revision, remember that one text-situation coupling or unit may be altered, discarded, or substituted without substantially affecting the rest.

We know very little about the actual oral delivery of Jesus and his contemporaries. But we know that oral delivery was structured to aid the memory. Repeating phrases and link phrases are memory devices. Excellent delivery in preaching can be achieved either with a complete manuscript (provided it is at least overlearned with key phrases memorized) or without. It is a good idea to go over the complete manuscript quickly seven or eight times out loud in front of a mirror to establish eye contact. The first two times may be to get a complete sense of the flow. The third and fourth times can be just to memorize the link phrases and the last few sentences. The final times should be looking into the eyes in the mirror as much as possible, with the last two times concentrating on gesture.

We know from oral cultures today how important gesture is in telling stories. It is interesting to ask an immigrant from an oral culture who speaks English as a second language to say something in his or her native tongue. Hand gestures absent in speaking English often accompany the switch. During the last couple of times of rehearsal, create some gestures—not a lot, but some, and have them varied. Good gestures always fall on a particular word and fit so naturally that they are almost unnoticed. Find out what that word is and perhaps draw a small stick figure in the margin to remind you of what the gesture is. Gestures with the arms need to be full, not just from the elbows. Most often, when we are rehearsing, we are geared toward the content. Try asking, "What is the feeling of this paragraph?" It is often the feelings that provide the gestures. *The aim in delivery is to think and feel the sermon or homily as we say it.* That is why reading does not work: if we are not having to think and feel as we go, our people will miss those natural pauses in our thought that help them understand what we are saying. Some things may be read, for instance a short quotation, but we should try to avoid reading a story. Stories are for telling.

What this amounts to is preaching as a carefully rehearsed event on Sunday morning. And of course it should be, When else can we visit so many people in such a short time? Perhaps we should remember too what the theater has always known: the most spontaneous and natural performance is the one that is most rehearsed. Mark Twain spoke for us all when he said, "I need to spend more time on my extemporaneous speeches."

CHAPTER SIX

SUNDAY

There is barely enough time. Sunday morning comes upon us through the steady rhythm of passing days, of lives struggling to live out the faith, of hope being born in the midst of it all, with a gracious predictability that preachers come to respect and love. What we end up with on Sunday is a word that has often been hard-won, whose disclosive truth the preacher reaches to grasp and hold onto even in the course of the preaching itself. All of the preacher's science and art, all of the technical skills and gifts with language, and all of the years of training and hours of public speaking, still do not add up to the sermon or homily. The Word that is proclaimed has a wondrous strangeness and mystery, even for the preacher, that marks it as God's Word, not the preacher's own.

We have been talking to this point about homiletical method in great detail, trying to identify rudimentary guidelines and suggestions as well as certain universals that might help begin to shape a homiletical grammar. The effect of the method here can be twofold: to assist us in preparing to preach and to provide us with language and analytical tools to explore what has gone on at foundational levels in any sermon or homily. In the final analysis, it matters less that we deviate from guidelines than that we use them to deepen our understanding of our task and of the reason something worked or did not work the way we anticipated. There are many ways to preach effectively. The approach developed here is one way that allows for great variety. Because it relies less on intuition than previous published approaches, it may help shed light on whatever approach or approaches we finally choose for ourselves.

For much of our journey, however, I have been doing in these pages what I have advocated against in preaching—I have been telling rather than showing, describing rather than creating. I am a strong believer that students and teachers working on preaching theory should be willing to allow their own preaching practice to come under scrutiny. I am now finding that my commitment to this idea is rather stronger when it involves others instead of myself. To include a sermon or homily of my own here means taking a risk. Preaching is, by its nature, quite personal, and individual styles vary greatly. Quite aside from personal vulnerability, I risk that readers might find apparent contradictions and dismiss the theory that has been developed in these pages: book sales will plummet, and I will be looking for a job. Moreover, a preached sermon or homily has already had its life and some of us believe that it is not to be analyzed academically. My head will rule over my heart on this matter however. There is value in seeing even just one example of what can be done using this approach.

A special occasion sermon or homily, preached in the congregation I was serving during much of the time that I wrote this book, will be used here. Commentary is provided. It is hoped that the reader's heart will be receptive to the manner in which I disregard some guidelines. These can be as instructive as experiencing other guidelines in practice. The congregation is large, middle-class, and suburban. It is Remembrance Sunday, November 9, 1986. The text is the gospel lesson assigned by the lectionary. It has little apparent connection with the day.

Luke 20:27-38. Some of the Sadducees, who say there is no resurrection, came to Jesus with a question. "Teacher," they said, "Moses wrote for us that if a man's brother dies and leaves a wife but no children, the man must marry the widow and have children for his brother. Now there were seven brothers. The first one married a woman and died childless. The second and then the third married her, and in the same way the seven died, leaving no children. Finally, the woman died too. Now then, at the resurrection whose wife will she be, since the seven were married to her?"

Jesus replied, "The people of this age marry and are given in marriage. But those who are considered worthy of taking part in that age and in the resurrection of the dead will neither marry nor be given in marriage, and they can no longer die; for they are like angels. They are God's children, since they are children of the resurrection. But in the account of the bush, even Moses showed that the dead rise, for he calls the Lord 'the God of Abraham, and the God of Isaac, and the God of Jacob.' He is not the God of the dead, but of the living, for to him all are alive."

Major concern of the text: All are alive to God.
The exegesis was done without regard to the Sunday occasion. This particular concern was selected to be the major concern of text afterward, when I considered Remembrance Day. There is an obvious connection to the deaths we remember. There is the potential for more spark than if I had chosen, for instance, to speak on the subject of marriage in the text.

Major concern of the sermon/homily: God remembers God's people.
This is a third transposition in order to use the word "remember." The first was "the dead are alive to God." The second was "God does not forget us."

Sermon/Homily

"Putting It Back Together Again"

Let me tell you about a picture that should have a place in my photo album. It is a picture perhaps like some of yours. It is taken from a boat looking toward the land. My Uncle Paul, after whom I am named, is standing on the dock he just built up at his cottage on Lake Huron last summer. He has on his red plaid work shirt and the old Eddie Bauer Safari pants.

The place is specific, the pants are a brand name. I will want to remember to address all the senses.

The sun is glinting off his bald head as he passes my son a glass of lemonade. My three cousins with whom I shrieked as a child on the old dock are setting off in the revarnished cedar canoe. Two of them are married now and have small children you can see on the pine-scented cottage paths where we used to play. And my Aunt Rose is on the porch kneeling by the spaniel they called Keel because the dog likes sailing.

My album is at best a ragtag affair, poorly kept, nourished infrequently. No matter how poor our albums, we all like looking at photos. We like remembering the goodness and the good times.

I am trying to name my feelings and the congregation's about what we have been doing.

I wish I had that photo, but it doesn't exist, except in my mind. You see, none of that exists. Not the family cottage, not the cousins and their children, not the dog named Keel, and not my Aunt Rose or my Uncle Paul. Because my Uncle was killed as a young man during wartime military exercises in Quebec before he even had a chance to marry. He fell under a moving train and all the way to his death he sang hymns in the ambulance to comfort my grandmother. I never met that uncle, or his brother, Uncle Ralph, who died in war-flight training. And none of our family has those loved ones or those memories we would like to have. The picture I do have is of my son, standing alone, at someone else's cottage.

I have told a personal story and now I shift the focus back to the congregation.

All of us have pictures that never made it into the family album because of the war. Stacks of pictures, hundreds of rolls of film.

We are already experiencing the law of Remembrance Day. Before going further I want to find a way of introducing either my major concern of the text or my major concern of the sermon/homily in order to indicate very early in the process where I am going.

We say, "Lest we forget." But it is hard to remember that God has not forgotten us; that God remembers God's people.

Major concern of the sermon/homily. I have used the exact wording. I have also used transposition 2, above, but this will only help communicate the thrust. Normally I do this earlier, sometime in the first paragraph. But that has not worked out this time. Stating the good news in this manner at this early stage does not give away the plot but simply serves to identify the theme in order that our people may be helped to listen. The idea of the photo album came from two directions. One was free-associating about the woman in the text whose husbands had died and remembering pictures a widow had shown me of her husband. The other was asking myself, since I was born after the war, how did the war affect me?

For many of us born during or after the Second World War, it has mostly seemed remote, unreal, a little like in Humpty Dumpty: "All the King's horses and all the King's men,/Couldn't put Humpty together again." What had we to do with it? Walter Kronkite cataloging the battles of the last war every Sunday afternoon, did not bring home its horror. Remembrance Day, with the parades and television broadcasts from the capital, the guns going off, always seemed as if it had something to do with us, but it was hard to make the connection. In school we would recite those words almost fiercely, as though they held the clue to the marching and the wreaths: "If ye break faith with us who die/We shall not sleep, though poppies grow/in Flanders fields." Seeing and knowing people our age killing and being killed in Vietnam made war more real but made Remembrance Day more ambiguous. How do we honor the dead from wars, without honoring war itself?

This is an issue for today.

For me the first time the Second World War was as real as today was in a trip to a graveyard near Dieppe in 1975. Grave after grave, the men from my country stretched dead along the ground as far as the distant windblown trees. And each marker had a tender inscription from loved ones back home, "to my son," "to my beloved husband," and so on . . . and so on. These dead suddenly were alive to me, although dead to future generations. For a few seconds, I felt like one of the relatives.

To this point narrative has been dominant and doctrine has been secondary. I am taking longer than usual to set the scene for the biblical text. Normally, I aim for an introductory paragraph, and then alternate paragraphs between textual focus and situational focus. But, as often happens, something is working on its own. In speaking of one-loop sermons or homilies we suggested that the first third might be a narrative. Although this is not a one-loop format, it is a form of that opening we are using here. Special occasion Sundays often mean the delayed entry of the text for me. I simply will need to be alert to give sufficient textual focus in what will remain of the law section.

The Sadducees approached Jesus in our gospel text. "Jesus," they might have said, "Jesus, you know that we are not like Pharisees—we do not believe in a resurrection of the dead. Nor are we like you in this regard. Therefore, kindly indulge us this one question on the matter. There was a woman whose husband died leaving her childless. She was forced by successive deaths and by law to marry seven brothers in succession. In the age to come, whose husband will she be?"

I have moved directly into the text without seeking a soft transition, as I might do at other times (i.e., "Our text today does not seem to have much to do with Remembrance Day.") Also, I am using direct speech to communicate some exegetical material and to remind the congregation of the scriptural passage.

It was a kind of shaggy-dog story, a riddle without an answer, meant to ridicule both the resurrection and Jesus.

The concern of the text from my exegesis needs little elaboration: The Pharisees told a riddle without an answer. The concern of the sermon/homily is: Some of our issues are shaggy-dog stories. The outstanding issue of Remembrance Day remains. Is there a way of developing this concern of the sermon/homily to zero in on Remembrance Day?

They might equally well have said to Jesus, "There were seven countries frequently at war. In the first battle the first country won. The second country won the second battle, the third won the third, and so on until each had won once. Tell us master," they might have asked Jesus, "in the resurrection of which you speak, which country will win the war?" Who *will* win the war in the next age? Will it be blacks or whites, males or females, homosexuals or heterosexuals, Americans or Russians? Whose wife will the woman be, the first husband's or the third? These are cool, distant questions, as impersonal as rock videos, as prodding as the bark of battlefield cannons.

I touch upon difficult issues here, but mention them only in passing and in a manner that may have at least a subliminal effect on the congregation this Sunday.

But if we took these questions seriously, as Jesus takes their questions seriously, we could find our heart's question. Jesus always goes to the questions of the heart. It is the heart's question that Jesus hears behind the riddles: How can God allow the suffering and loss of war? How can God look on any suffering? How could God allow such suffering that a woman should have to marry seven brothers? Or that she should be deemed worthless seven times simply because she bore no children? Or that she should have to bury seven husbands? Or that parents should bury several children, or that there should be rape and murder and disease? How can you allow this God? Have you forgotten us? Remember us we pray on this Remembrance Day.

This is further naming what might be our issues on the day. The concern of the text here is: Jesus takes their questions seriously. The concern of the sermon is: Jesus takes our questions seriously. They are developed simultaneously in this paragraph. I am now a little more than halfway. It is time to shift into good news with concentrated treatment of the major concern of the text and major concern of the sermon/homily. The previous sentence is the link phrase. We are now at the reversal point. Gospel will be the focus now.

God has never forgotten us. God remembers God's people. God is God of the living. But God in Christ turns the question back to us. Through the words of our text, as Christ goes on to answer the Pharisees, we can hear God saying to us, How can you people, children of God, allow such things to happen? Remember me. I am God of the living, not God of the dead. There is no longer any need to forge armaments, for you may trust in me—the amount you spend in two weeks on weapons could bring fresh water, food, and shelter to all the people of this world. You could change life on this planet. Surely you have already lost too much in war.

This difficult issue is raised in an invitational, good news way. The educational program of the church on this occasion had taken responsibility for doing in-depth teaching on the subject of peace.

There is no power in death. There is no power in your ruling over the dead. Those who want a God of the graveyard may find another God. I am the God of life. Those who want a God who wills war may find another God. I am the God of life. Those who want a God who likes to see suffering may find another God. I am the God of life. And because of this, I go to the places of death, to the heartache of the widow, to the agony of the emergency ward, to the despair of the broken family, to the ghettos of suffering of the poor, to raise them up and to bring forth fullness. Into each of your lives, God says, I am reaching to bring blessings. No turmoil is too great, no loneliness is too deep, no longing is too much, no hunger is too ravenous, no tears are too plenteous, no injury is too serious, no disease so dangerous, no pain is so piercing, no sin is so huge, that I cannot bring life. My way is the way of resurrection and eternal life. Even the dead are alive to

me, for to me all are alive. For to me all are alive.
Marriage is of this age, but in my age you will all
be united as one family even as I already unite you
as the one body of Christ. Wars and fighting are of
this age, but in my age there is no war and there
are no victors in war.

This concludes development of my major concern of the
text. I have given sufficient textual and exegetical material to
support it. While it is not necessary to do so, I have again used
direct speech in order to keep the presented material lively
and to ensure that there is no seam between doctrine and
narrative. Pastoral and prophetic have been balanced. The
major concern of the sermon/homily will now be developed
with stories I have heard from conversations with members of
the congregation.

God remembers us and has remembered us in
the past. We have not been destroyed by death.
We have not been overcome by war. On this day
we remember—and this is surely one of the
purposes of Remembrance Day—that we are a
people capable of great destruction.

This idea has the effect of law and therefore I do not go on
to develop it here.

But on this day we also remember that we are a
people capable of acts of great love and kindness
and bravery. We think of women who fought the
war raising children alone or who waited by the
sea for a loved one who never returned. I think of
the story of the rear gunner who shouted through
the radio that he was trapped and couldn't bail
out, and whose captain stayed in the plane and
said back to him, "It's all right, son, we will go
down on this one together." We think of people
being kind to one another in spite of the war, like
the Allied and Nazi troops who fought one

another by day, but whose humanity won out at night as they traded rations with one another. We think of God who gave his son, Jesus Christ, that even in our darkest times, there might be light. And we think of the continued actions of congregations such as this one in aiding families who have had to flee from wars in other lands. God remembers us.

For the second time the Christ-event has been mentioned. In order that God's action not seem remote, the congregation's refugee program is noted. It also serves to invite the congregation to further action. It is time to end the sermon. To do this I will return to the opening remarks and come back again to the major concern of text and the major concern of sermon/homily.

No, I do not have the picture of our extended family. It is only a picture of my son on someone else's dock. But I do have family pictures, even as you have wonderful pictures of your families.

I want the focus to be on their lives.

We have them at great price. The other pictures we do not have, but God has them. As Jesus says, "[God] is not God of the dead, but of the living, for to [God] all are alive." The word "remember" means to make members again, to put together again.

This is perhaps not a good time to introduce a new idea, but it seems to work toward the conclusion here.

And it is this God who remembers us, who will bring us all back together as one, even as it happens in this moment and in the age to come.

Conclusion

We have come a long way with imagination of the heart and there still is much more for all of us to explore and learn. I have argued here that imagination for preaching is not simply the ability to think in pictures, it is a function of language. As such it is a skill that can be developed. Tools that will assist it can be taught and learned. Since language is our primary tool as preachers, it falls to us to use language to the utmost of our ability to communicate God's Word.

It has not been possible to do this without going deeply into the structure of language to see how meaning is generated between poles. I have argued that imagination is simply a heightened act of meaning and that imagination of the heart is that form of imagination peculiar to the Christian. It is imagination leavened by both scripture and experience. To show how to use imagination effectively we have had to go deeply into the structure of biblical preaching as well, isolating four key and universal polarities in the preaching task: biblical text and our situation; law and gospel (or judgment and grace); story and doctrine; and finally, pastor and prophet. To try to address them all at once is impossible for us, but since there is a natural and sequential order to them, if we address each one a day at a time, we incorporate them from the beginning of the preaching task. We end up with sparks at several different levels as the preaching takes place. What we have been talking about is *biblical preaching* and each of these many sparks has its origin in the biblical text and tradition. In fact, it is our hope that the biblical text to a large degree has dictated the entire preaching event, or, said another way, that the sermon or homily has in part written itself.

Talking about preaching without talking about method is like putting someone in a canoe for the first time without a demonstration of how to paddle. Thus we have also attempted to begin to develop a language with which we can talk about method. The guidelines for biblical preaching outlined here provide a basis for that language. Concepts such as concern of the text and concern of the sermon (or concern of the homily), text-situation units, law and gospel, reversal, loops, sparks, story and doctrine, pastor and prophet, and so forth, are applicable to any preaching, whatever our approach, at least as a starting point for discussion. They have been developed here for preachers who seek better control of their own creative abilities, better ability to understand how others are achieving what they are, and better ways to critique what we and others do.

We have long recognized that preaching has an art to it. We are more recently coming to recognize that some forms of preaching are art, functioning along principles similar to those found in other forms of art. Developments in homiletics-related disciplines, for instance in biblical interpretation, as well as some of what we have been doing here, may indicate something else—that preaching has a science to it as well. It is a science that in part is attentive to structures in language. When we make structure conscious, we make control of meaning conscious. And when we have conscious control of meaning we also have an ability to use imagination freely for powerful effect.

Fine preaching is like a stained-glass window;

we are not so much aware of the lead structure as we are of the beauty of the light that shines through the glass. A motive that has lurked behind these pages is language renewal for the renewal of faith. Preachers hold up the words of the faith in order that the light of Christ will color where we walk. This is a large part of the excitement of preaching, sharing in the new reality that the language of faith keeps disclosing. Dylan Thomas once told actors rehearsing *Under Milk Wood* to "listen to the words—love the words." If we can help our people see the language of the faith as beautiful and exciting again, if we can help them find the spark of light glimmering through seemingly opaque Bible passages, and if we can share our own joy in God's Word speaking to all dimensions of contemporary life, with the help of the Holy Spirit, we will have succeeded in offering the invitation to faith.

The notion of prophecy as the dreaming of alternate realities is appropriate for imagination. What if we were to do as Luke did, and see the Holy Spirit active everywhere the disciples went? Or what if we were occasionally to claim for our church the extravagant miracles Luke does for his church at the beginning of Acts—an extravagance that testifies to the fullness and completeness of his faith? What if we were to see this world more frequently with the eyes of faith? Is this not what Jesus encouraged, for instance in speaking of faith moving mountains? Is this not what Martin Luther King did in speaking of having been to the mountaintop? And is this not what Winnie Mandela and Bishop Tutu are doing in South Africa? If we do this, will we not be speaking the truth that counts? Will we not be speaking a truth that, far from being oblivious to historical truth, confesses it and puts it in the proper perspective? Will the world not start to look a little different? And will we and our people not be able to start seeing more clearly the Realm of God breaking in?

This is not idle dreaming. It is prophetic dreaming. It is an invitation for us to use our faith and understanding of language more completely to shape our preaching. It is an invitation for us to develop a theology of language. What we are talking about is, of course, what we have been talking about all along. It is in the tension between different ideas, the world as it is and the world as God in Christ is enabling it to become, that imagination and faith can find room to move. And it is by paying attention to the poles in language that metaphors for faith are created. In our current age we often speak of the need for renewal of faith, recognizing that it is something that must happen over and over again, even as we must be converted over and over again, even as language lives and language dies. As preachers we are in a special way custodians of language for the world God created and loves without ceasing.

N O T E S

Chapter 1/Imagination's Poles

1. Søren Kierkegaard, *Concluding Unscientific Postscript*, trans. D. F. Swenson and W. Lowrie (Princeton, N. J.: Princeton University Press, 1941), p. 315.

2. It has been used positively already by Elizabeth Achtemeier and James Breech, as will be seen later, as well as by Charles L. Bartow in *The Preaching Moment* (Nashville: Abingdon Press, 1980), pp. 33 ff.

3. Walther Eichrodt, *Theology of the Old Testament*, vol. 2, trans. J. A. Baker (Philadelphia: Westminster Press, 1967), p. 143.

4. Gerhard Ebeling, *The Nature of Faith*, trans. Ronald G. Smith (Philadelphia: Muhlenburg Press, 1962), p. 102.

5. Cited by Edward F. Markquart, *Quest for Better Preaching* (Minneapolis: Augsburg, 1985), p. 160.

6. Ralph W. Sockman, *The Highway of God* (New York: Macmillan, 1942), p. 209.

7. Arndt L. Halvorson, *Authentic Preaching* (Minneapolis: Augsburg, 1982), p. 119.

8. The Bishop's Committee on Priestly Life and Ministry, *Fulfilled in Your Hearing* (U. S. Catholic, 1982), p. 25.

9. Fred B. Craddock, *As One Without Authority* (Nashville: Abingdon Press, 1971), p. 78.

10. Charles Rice in *Preaching Biblically*, ed. Don Wardlaw (Philadelphia: Westminster Press, 1983), p. 104.

11. See Halvorson, *Authentic Preaching*, p. 119, and Markquart, *Quest for Better Preaching*, p. 163.

12. David Buttrick, *Homiletic: Moves and Structures* (Philadelphia: Fortress Press, 1987), p. 116.

13. See Walter J. Ong, S.J., *Ramus: Method, and the Decay of Dialogue* (Cambridge, Mass.: Harvard University Press, 1958). See also Mary E. Lyons, "Homiletics and Rhetoric: Recognizing an Ancient Alliance," *Homiletic*, XII, 1, pp. 1-4.

14. Sallie McFague, *Speaking in Parables* (Philadelphia: Fortress Press, 1975), p. 79.

15. Elizabeth Achtemeier, *Creative Preaching* (Nashville: Abingdon Press, 1980), p. 31.

16. Clyde E. Fant, ed., *Bonhoeffer: Worldly Preaching* (Nashville: Thomas Nelson, 1915), pp. 26, 70-73, 136.

17. See Reuel Howe, *Partners in Preaching* (New York: Seabury Press, 1967).

18. Bartow, *The Preaching Moment*.

19. See Paul Scott Wilson, "Coleridge, Leigh Hunt, Hazlitt, and Lamb: An Examination of Their Evolving Ideas of Imagination in Relation to Their Dramatic and Shakespearean Criticism." Ph.D. thesis, King's College, University of London, 1978.

20. See Eugene A. Nida's treatment of Pierce in his *Componential Analysis of Meaning* (The Hague: Mouton, 1975).

21. See, for instance, Sallie McFague, *Metaphorical Theology* (Philadelphia: Fortress Press, 1982), especially pp. 38 ff.

22. Roman Jakobson and Morris Halle, *Fundamentals of Language* (The Hague: Mouton, 1956). See especially pp. 34 ff.

23. See Claude Levi-Strauss, *The Savage Mind* (London: Weidenfeld & Nicolson, 1966).

24. Terry Eagleton, *Literary Theory: An Introduction* (Minneapolis: University of Minnesota Press, 1983), p. 104.

25. See, for instance, the discussion of oppositions *and* contradictions (or negations) in A. J. Greimas, *Du Sens* (Paris: Seuil, 1970), pp. 135 ff.

26. See Paul Ricoeur, *The Rule of Metaphor* (Toronto: University of Toronto Press, 1977), especially pp. 120 ff.

27. Markquart, *Quest for Better Preaching*, p. 32.

28. Arthur Koestler, *Act of Creation* (New York: Macmillan, 1964).

29. Frederick Buechner, *Telling the Truth* (New York: Harper & Row, 1977), p. 63.

30. Other polarities that we could name, such as individual/social, subjective/objective, and immanent/transcendent, may be addressed through these four.

Chapter 2/The Biblical Text and Our Situation

1. David Tracy, *Blessed Rage for Order* (New York: Seabury Press, 1975), pp. 43 ff.

2. William Skudlarek, *The Word in Worship* (Nashville: Abingdon Press, 1981), pp. 39-40.

3. Lectionary preachers should be aware of the unintentional distortion of some of the lectionary texts simply because of the primacy given to Gospel texts, because of the passages alongside the texts to be chosen to be read, and because of decisions about the length of selected passages. Justo and Catherine González have documented a number of examples concerning length. See *Liberation Preaching* (Nashville: Abingdon Press, 1980), p. 38 ff. The *Common Lectionary: The Lectionary Proposed by the Consultation on Common Texts* (New York: The Church Hymnal Corporation, 1983) documents other considerations. The lectionary, for those who use it, is a gift to the church, not an idol—some flexibility in its handling is necessary.

4. James Breech, ed., in his "Preface" to Amos Wilder's *Jesus' Parables and the War of Myths* (Philadelphia: Fortress Press, 1982), p. 6.

5. Ibid., p. 2.

6. Thomas H. Troeger, "Shaping Sermons by the Encounter of Text with Preacher," in *Preaching Biblically*, ed. Don Wardlaw (Philadelphia: Westminster Press, 1983), p. 155.

7. Eugene L. Lowry, *Doing Time in the Pulpit* (Nashville: Abingdon Press, 1985), p. 99.

8. Fred B. Craddock, *Preaching* (Nashville: Abingdon Press, 1985), pp. 78-80.

9. Leander E. Keck, *The Bible in the Pulpit* (Nashville: Abingdon Press, 1978), p. 63.

10. Thomas G. Long, "Shaping Sermons by Plotting the

Text's Claim upon Us," in *Preaching Biblically*, p. 89.

11. Arthur Koestler, *Act of Creation* (New York: Macmillan, 1964).

12. Martin Marty in *At the Edge of Hope*, eds. Howard Butt and Elliot Wright (New York: Seabury Press, 1978), p. 177.

13. Keck, *The Bible in the Pulpit*, pp. 53 ff. and 105.

14. For more on this see Ernest Best, *From Text to Sermon* (Atlanta, Ga.: John Knox Press, 1978), pp. 14 ff.

15. Keck, *The Bible in the Pulpit*, p. 14.

16. See Martin Marty in *At the Edge of Hope*, pp. 175-77.

17. Helmut Gollwitzer, *An Introduction to Protestant Theology* (Philadelphia: Westminster Press, 1978), p. 60.

18. Justo and Catherine González provide five helpful guidelines to what they call the "hermeneutic of suspicion" with a biblical text: (a) ask questions of power concerning who is "inside," in authority, and who is "outside," and also how God responds to power and powerlessness; (b) shift from identifying with the characters we normally identify with and see what the text means now; (c) imagine reading the text in a situation radically different from our own, for instance as a poor person; (d) seek out the justice component of the text for its day and translate that, not the specific message for that day, into our situation; and (e) finally, avoid avoiding the difficult issues the texts raise and which modern commentators often choose to avoid. See *Liberation Preaching*, pp. 69-93.

19. Richard Lischer, *A Theology of Preaching* (Nashville: Abingdon Press, 1981), pp. 62-63.

20. Keck, *The Bible in the Pulpit*, p. 101.

21. Elizabeth Achtemeier, *Creative Preaching* (Nashville: Abingdon Press, 1980), p. 46.

22. Further theoretical support for this claim of universality I have recently discovered in Harold T. Bryson and James C. Taylor, *Building Sermons to Meet People's Needs* (Nashville: Broadman Press, 1980), pp. 52-68, whom I will discuss here under "Reversal Point and the Central Idea."

Chapter 3/Law and Gospel

1. Gerhard Ebeling, *Luther: An Introduction to His Thought* (Philadelphia: Fortress Press, 1970), p. 113.

2. One of the best books on the subject for systematic theology is Gerhard O. Forde's, *The Law-Gospel Debate* (Minneapolis: Augsburg, 1969).

3. Herman Stuempfle, *Preaching Law and Gospel* (Philadelphia: Fortress Press, 1978).

4. Ebeling, *Luther: An Introduction to His Thought*, p. 117.

5. Walter Brueggemann, "Covenant as Subversive Paradigm," *Christian Century*, Nov. 12, 1980, p. 1096.

6. Dominic Grasso, S.J., *Proclaiming God's Message* (Notre Dame: University of Notre Dame Press, 1965), p. 200.

7. Ibid., p. 19.

8. Edward Schillebeeckx, *Jesus* (New York: Seabury Press, 1979), p. 105.

9. Stuempfle, *Preaching Law and Gospel*, pp. 21 ff.

10. Ibid., p. 29.

11. Martin Luther, "Table Talk" (1531), *Luther's Works* (Philadelphia: Fortress Press, 1955), 54, p. 127.

12. Richard Lischer, *A Theology of Preaching* (Nashville: Abingdon Press, 1981), p. 57.

13. Edmund A. Steimle, Morris J. Niedenthal, and Charles L. Rice, *Preaching the Story* (Philadelphia: Fortress Press, 1980), p. 148.

14. Ibid. p. 149.

15. Milton Crum, Jr., *Manual on Preaching* (Valley Forge, Pa.: Judson Press, 1977), p. 19.

16. Ibid., see pp. 19-71.

17. Eugene L. Lowry, *The Homiletical Plot: The Sermon as Narrative Art Form* (Atlanta: John Knox, 1980).

18. Robert P. Waznak, *Sunday After Sunday: Preaching the Homily as Story* (Mahwah, N.J.: Paulist Press, 1983), pp. 108-9.

19. Deane A. Kemper, *Effective Preaching: A Manual for Students and Pastors* (Philadelphia: Westminster Press, 1985), pp. 58 ff.

20. Eugene L. Lowry has a similar concept of reversal, less rooted in law-gospel. See *The Homiletical Plot*, pp. 48 ff.

21. John Killinger, *Fundamentals of Preaching* (Philadelphia: Fortress Press, 1985), pp. 44-46.

22. James W. Cox, *Preaching* (New York: Harper & Row, 1985), pp. 86-87.

23. Killinger, *Fundamentals of Preaching*, p. 44.

24. Fred B. Craddock, *Preaching* (Nashville: Abingdon Press, 1985), p. 157.

25. Harold T. Bryson and James C. Taylor, *Building Sermons to Meet People's Needs* (Nashville: Broadman Press, 1980), pp. 52-68.

26. Elizabeth Achtemeier, *The Old Testament and the Proclamation of the Gospel* (Philadelphia: Westminster Press, 1973).

Chapter 4/Story and Doctrine

1. Benjamin Franklin, *Autobiography and Other Writings* (Boston: Houghton Mifflin, 1958), pp. 74-75.

2. Cited by Charles Rice, "The Preacher as Storyteller," *USQR*, vol. XXX1, 3, Spring 1976, p. 191.

3. A. E. Garvie, *A Guide to Preachers* (London: Hodder & Stoughton, 1906), pp. 239, 242.

4. William F. Lynch, S. J., *Christ and Apollo: The Dimensions of the Literary Imagination* (New York: New American Library, 1963), p. 23.

5. Sallie McFague, *Metaphorical Theology* (Philadelphia: Fortress Press, 1982).

6. Stephen Crites, "The Narrative Quality of Experience," *JAAR*, 39, 1971, pp. 291 ff.

7. Hints of this may be found, for instance, in Alton H. McEachern, "Narrative Preaching," in *Preaching in Today's World*, comp. James C. Barry (Nashville: Broadman Press, 1984), pp. 151-57; and in James Earl Massey, *Designing the Sermon* (Nashville: Abingdon Press, 1980), pp. 35-49.

8. Garvie, *A Guide to Preachers*, p. 235.

9. Ibid., p. 229.

10. John Killinger, *Fundamentals of Preaching* (Philadelphia: Fortress Press, 1985), pp. 108-9.

11. James Breech, *The Silence of Jesus* (Philadelphia: Fortress Press, 1983), p. 217.

12. William H. Willimon, "Stories and Sermons: A Look at Preaching as Storytelling," *Christian Ministry*, 14, 6, 1983, pp. 5-7.

13. Robert P. Waznak, *Sunday After Sunday: Preaching the Homily as Story* (Mahwah, N. J.: Paulist Press, 1983).

14. Those interested in a comprehensive review of this literature should consult Edgar Henneche, *New Testament Apocrypha*, 2 vols. (Philadelphia: Westminster Press, 1966) and Ron Cameron, ed., *The Other Gospels* (Philadelphia: Westminster Press, 1982). For a brief account see, for instance, C. H. Henkey in *New Catholic Encyclopedia*, 1967, II, 404-14.

15. See W. H. C. Frend, *Martyrdom and Persecution in the Early Church* (New York: Doubleday, 1967).

16. Hans Frei, *The Eclipse of Biblical Narrative* (New Haven: Yale University Press, 1974).

17. A. C. Baugh, *A Literary History of England* (New York: Appleton-Century-Crofts, 1948), p. 273.

18. Waznak, *Sunday After Sunday*, p. 28.

19. See the work and influence of Milton Erickson, *My Voice Will Go with You* (New York: W. W. Norton, 1982) in which the importance of story in altering the unconscious has been stressed.

20. See Johann Metz, *Faith in History and Society* (New York: Seabury Press, 1980), and Robert J. Schreiter, *Constructing Local Theologies* (New York: Orbis Books, 1985).

21. See Peter Slater, *The Dynamics of Religion* (New York: Harper & Row, 1978).

22. Gabriele Rico, *Writing the Natural Way* (Los Angeles: T. P. Archer, 1983).

23. Fred B. Craddock, *Preaching* (Nashville: Abingdon Press, 1985), pp. 173-74.

24. Ibid., p. 123.

25. H. Grady Davis, *Design for Preaching* (Philadelphia: Fortress Press, 1958), pp. 265 ff; Charles L. Bartow, *The Preaching Moment* (Nashville: Abingdon Press, 1980), pp. 36-46, 69-89; Thomas H. Troeger, *Creating Fresh Images for Preaching* (Valley Forge, Pa.: Judson Press, 1982).

26. Henry H. Mitchell, *The Recovery of Preaching* (New York: Harper & Row, 1977), pp. 45-73; Bruce A. Rosenburg, *The Art of the American Folk Preacher* (New York: Oxford University Press, 1970), pp. 35-95.

27. One of the first people to advocate this kind of format was Charles L. Rice, *Interpretation and Imagination* (Philadelphia: Fortress Press, 1970), pp. 84 ff. and lately Eugene Lowry, *The Homiletical Plot* (Atlanta: John Knox Press, 1980), Waznak, *Sunday After Sunday*, and Fred Baumer, "Unlocking the Imagination," in Frank McNulty's *Preaching Better* (Mahwah, N. J.: Paulist Press, 1985), pp. 80-86, have spoken of related forms.

Chapter 5/Pastor and Prophet

1. Ronald H. Sunderland in *The Pastor as Servant*, eds. Earl E. Shelp and Ronald H. Sunderland (New York: Pilgrim Press, 1986), p. 37.

2. Daniel L. Migliore, in *The Pastor as Prophet*, eds. Earl E. Shelp and Ronald H. Sutherland (New York: Pilgrim Press, 1985), p. 130.

3. John Dominic Crossan, *In Parables* (New York: Harper & Row, 1973), p. 35.

4. C. S. Song, *Tell Us Our Names: Story Theology from an Asian Perspective* (Maryknoll, N. Y.: Orbis Books, 1984), p. 16.

5. Marianne H. Micks, *The Future Present* (New York: Seabury Press, 1970), p. 177.

6. Robert McAfee Brown, *Theology in a New Key* (Philadelphia: Westminster, 1978), p. 13.

7. John H. Westerhoff, in *Social Themes of the Christian Year*, ed. Deiter T. Hessel (Geneva Press, 1983), p. 18.

8. Walter Brueggemann, *The Prophetic Imagination* (Philadelphia: Fortress Press, 1978), p. 110.

9. Stanley M. Hauerwas, in *The Pastor as Prophet*, p. 43.

10. Northrop Frye, *Creation and Recreation* (Toronto: University of Toronto Press, 1980), pp. 18-19.

11. Brueggemann, *The Prophetic Imagination*, p. 45.

12. Walter Brueggemann, in *The Pastor as Prophet*, pp. 51-52.

13. In addition to denominational resources, consider books such as Hessel's *Social Themes of the Christian Year*.

14. David Buttrick, *Homiletic: Moves and Structures* (Philadelphia: Fortress Press, 1987), p. 430.

15. Frederick Buechner, *Telling the Truth: The Gospel as Tragedy, Comedy, and Fairy Tale* (New York: Harper & Row, 1977), p. 21.

16. Fred B. Craddock, *Overhearing the Gospel* (Nashville: Abingdon Press, 1978).

17. Richard A. Jensen, *Telling the Story* (Minneapolis: Augsburg, 1980), p. 139.

18. Sallie McFague, *Speaking in Parables* (Philadelphia: Fortress Press, 1975), p. 16. She is drawing on Philip Wheelwright's terms.

19. Johann Metz, *Faith in History and Society* (New York: Seabury Press, 1980), p. 162.

20. Robert Schreiter, *Constructing Local Theologies* (Maryknoll, N. Y.: Orbis Books, 1985).

21. Roger Hutchinson and Gibson Winter, "Towards a Method in Political Ethics," in *Perspectives on Political Ethics: An Ecumenical Enquiry*, ed. Koson Sprisong (New York: World Council of Churches and Georgetown University, 1983), p. 164.

22. Stanley Hauerwas, *A Community of Character: Toward a Constructive Christian Social Ethic* (Notre Dame: University of Notre Dame, 1981), pp. 145-52.

23. Dan Otto Via, Jr., *The Parables: Their Literary and Existential Dimension* (Philadelphia: Fortress Press, 1967), p. 172.

24. Eta Linnemann, *Parables of Jesus: Introduction and Exposition* (London: S.P.C.K., 1966), pp. 24 ff.

25. James Breech, *The Silence of Jesus* (Philadelphia: Fortress Press, 1983), p. 213.

26. The Good Samaritan and the Prodigal Son may be possible exceptions, along with allegorical passages such as Matthew 22:1-14 or Matthew 23:37, for they have details embedded within them which, it may be argued, demand religious interpretation.

27. See Breech, *The Silence of Jesus*, p. 75.

28. See Kenneth E. Bailey, *Through Peasant Eyes* (Grand Rapids: Wm. B. Eerdmans, 1980), p. 24 ff.

29. Breech, *The Silence of Jesus*, p. 212.

30. Fred B. Craddock, unpublished paper delivered at the Toronto School of Theology, June, 1986.

31. See Rudolph Bultmann, *History of the Synoptic Tradition*, trans. John Marsh (New York: Harper & Row, 1963), pp. 188-92.

32. Tom Troeger is a poet who has managed to use this form well in his *Creating Fresh Images for Preaching* (Valley Forge, Pa.: Judson Press, 1982).

33. The author W. P. Kinsella's numerous collections of short stories focusing on the North American Indian are poignant examples of raising tough issues while not losing the ability to laugh.

34. Gary D. Stratman, *Pastoral Preaching: Timeless Truth for Changing Needs* (Nashville: Abingdon Press, 1983), pp. 64-66.

I N D E X